**CORNWALL COUNTY COUNCIL
LIBRARIES AND ARTS DEPARTMENT**

BACK-A-LONG

ISABEL PICKERING

**Some Memories of the
People of Polruan and the
Parish of Lanteglos-by-Fowey**

Copyright 1997 by Isabel Pickering

ISBN 0-9521980-3-7
British Library Cataloguing-in-Publication Data
A Catalogue record for this book is available from the British Library

First Published 1997

Published by ISABEL PICKERING
Lescrow Farm, Passage Lane, Fowey, Cornwall PL23 1JS

Produced by John Thomlinson, Polruan, Cornwall

© Illustrated by Margaret Taylor, Polruan, Cornwall

Printed by Trevedda Press, Lanteglos-by-Fowey, Cornwall

Hand Bound by Peter Lane, Liskeard, Cornwall

1753
-

Acknowledgements

I would like to extend my heartfelt thanks to all those who helped me write this book. To the many people who shared their memories with me through the years, to my husband, Bob, who encouraged me and left me free for so many, many hours to visit and listen to so many older people of the parish. To Barbara Guernier and John Thomlinson who gave me invaluable advice and proof-read tirelessly, to Margaret Taylor, who provided the charming illustrations, and to my son, Philip, who helped me when I was mired down in computor technology. Without all of you this book would not have been possible and would have remained an untidy bundle of notes in a box. Thank you again, so much.

Introduction

In the past few years I have tried to give you, the people of the parish of Lanteglos, a record of some of the best of the pictures you have so kindly lent me, as well as part of your history contained in a collection of news stories of the nineteenth century.

Now I have collected a selection of memories some of you have generously shared with me. Those who allowed me to take a tape recording of what they were saying, can be clearly heard through the very words they used. Others, who preferred me to write down their recollections, have their reminiscences unavoidably written more in my wording. Nevertheless, all of these are how those people remembered earlier days in the parish.

I have been fascinated to learn of this world of bygone Lanteglos-by-Fowey. I hope you will be able to relive these earlier days and enjoy this travel back in time as much as I have.

ISABEL PICKERING

Contents

Sidney Ball
BORN IN 1887, SPEAKING IN 1987

My father was born Rilla Mill. There were three or four mills on the same stream there. Father decided to leave and go with a big company at St. Austell as manager. There he met a farmer's daughter, Elizabeth Dunn, and married her.

As a young child, before school age, I remember sitting in the mill by the stairs watching the flour being ground by the millstone and being carried by conveyor up into the centrifugal.

Father had one of the last of the old water-wheel flour mills at Trethake. Farmers brought their grain to us to grind. After threshing they would come and make a deal with Father. A firm, Belbin, near Southampton sent a cargo of roller-made flour to Fowey. That squashed Father's business completely - he couldn't compete with roller-made flour. He had to stop the flour business. After the roller-made flour came in. we still kept a business selling cattle feed. and I had a coal store at Pont.

Farming was completely different then, a different world a hundred years ago. Then it was all by hand. When I went to school. I remember a dear old lady, Mary Ann Wyatt. She was eighty. and in the Spring she would go up to Tredudwell to Mr. Allchin to weed the violets. Do you know how much she was paid to do that? Half a crown a week. And she had to take any children with her.

We kept a dairy - seven cows - we used the extra milk to feed the pigs. The pigs went to Tiverton or Redruth factory when they were ready. When we were feeding the pigs, we had to shut them up; but when they were being reared, they were out with their mothers. Pig feeding was usually early autumn. We didn't feed them summer times. The weather was so hot then, it would go poor.

Market days were nothing special to us - it was all in the day's work. We went to market to Lostwithiel or Liskeard. At one time, before lorries, we drove the pigs to market. One time Mr. Kendall had ten or twenty which he brought to us, then we drove them all together. We took a horse and cart to pick up any who dropped out. That was to Lostwithiel.

We had a vegetable garden, of course. We grew beautiful currants, gooseberries, potatoes, beans, the lot.

I started school when I was six. It was a four mile walk to school and another four mile back. Miss Slade was my first teacher. She was a small woman, very nice. My next teacher was a man, Sidney Whitten. That was in Standards I and II. I went to school until I was sixteen, and had private tuition from the schoolmaster because he was a friend. This had to stop in the 1914-1918 War. You see, they took the men. My sister and I had to do all we could to help at home. Father was eighty and retired.

An old man used to come from Fowey, a witty old chap, with a bundle and a little case. He'd travel the country side-peddling clothing. I dearly liked him; he was witty. "You buy feathers, and I buy tick. And we'll be married very quick." He'd come in, put his bundle on the table, undo it and tip out everything for us to choose. He had everything in that bundle, both for boys and girls. He was a tall, upright man.

Christmas was strictly a family affair. Of course, we looked forward to it. There were always special things prepared - cakes, dinner. We always decorated with holly, and a Christmas tree, fir, with tinsel and things you tied on, bells etc.

Then there were the Darkey Parties - everyone would dress up in all kinds of dress - hats, feathers. There was considerable dressing up. They would smoke their faces. Then they would play the tambourine, concertina, and bones. To play the bones you took two ribs of horse or bullock, about seven inches long, and held them between the fingers of one hand, two in the other hand the same way and click them together (like some play spoons today). They went from house to house, at each played several tunes. We never had them come inside.

For clothes for us all, a private dressmaker used to go around the farm places

8

to do all their sewing. She'd stop a week at a time on a farm to do the sewing for everyone in the house. I was a naughty little rascal - wouldn't let her put anything on me. She lived at Highway, but I don't remember her name.

For shoes we went to Mr. Simmons in Polruan, to both Mr. Simmonses, both down at the little shop and later when he moved up the street to the larger shop.

On the farm to protect ourselves from the rain, we always used a sack over our shoulders, never waterproofs. I don't remember any Wellingtons.

When the Great Blizzard came in 1891, I remember my Father telling me about it. The thing was, it lasted such a long time. People in Polperro were starving. Nothing could get to them by sea or by land. Father gathered a lot of men and shovelled his way to the village, took flour to the Polperro bakers. They were really starving; it lasted so long, you see. It lasted three weeks and the sheep were buried for three weeks. But they didn't die; they managed to feed on earth and the bits of green under the snow. When they were finally rescued they had lost the use of their legs and couldn't walk. It took three weeks of the blizzard to do that to them, and it took three weeks for them to recover after. But they did recover!

Father and Mother were disciplinarians absolutely. They couldn't send us children to Sunday School, but they had Bibles. We always had Sunday Bible readings in our own home. The British and Foreign Bible Society Bibles, I can see them now in the kitchen window.

SARAH TRUSCOTT SWIGGS
BORN IN 1890, SPEAKING IN 1980

Farming in the 1890's was far different to what it is today. It was all hard work then, from daylight till dark. When I was very young, I started doing things on the farm before I went to school and after I came back. I used to feed the young chickens, because in those days the farmer's wife had a lot of poultry to look after. The more she kept, the more money she had to run the home with.

Also she milked as many cows as she could to make as much butter as she could to get money to run the house with. And in those days everything indoors and out was done by hand. We sat on a three-legged stool to milk the cows, and many a time if the cows caught her teat in a bramble and scratched it, she would kick you off your stool. You had to pull yourself together again and get on again. It was all work and no play for many years, and yet we were happy in our work.

We milked the cows by hand, strained the milk through pieces of muslin into a pan, then let it stay till next day, then scald it next day, skimmed the cream off, and made it into butter. At the time I am talking about, there were no separator churns.

10

We used to be up early while it was cool and make the butter before the cream got hot - summer time I am talking about now. But the butter tasted lovely then. It was the real thing. How different it tastes now!

I well remember when we first had a separator and churn to make the butter. We couldn't believe it could be done, but after that things were getting different. I well remember many many years of the hard work it was. But we were happy doing it because we were used to it.

Now about rearing calves. They were kept on the mother for a week or so. Then we weaned them. That was work too. We had to put our hand in their mouth and in the milk. It took a lot of time and patience. We had bites with their sharp little teeth. It took a long time too, but it had to be done.

Of course, we had every kind of fruit, orchards with plenty of apples, pears, and plums. We always made plenty of jam and jelly. We were never without a job. But it was lovely to go out and gather all the fruit we needed. It was well worth doing all the work that was attached to it.

And when the days got short there was plenty of knitting and sewing to be done by candle-light and small oil lamps. When we wanted to go to another room in the dark evenings, we had to light a candle. No electric to turn on whichever room you wanted to go in.

Take sanitary conditions then. There was no sanitation indoors. We had to go outdoors in a little shack with only a bucket, which had to be emptied. No one grumbled about it because they knew it wouldn't make any difference. When I hear and see what is going on today, I can't understand it. No one seems satisfied.

All these things had to be done before we did any homework. That had to be done later. Our own bread and cake had to be made and baked sometimes, not buying like we do now. It was all plain living - no fancies like now. And I am sure the plain food was better for health.

But we always looked on Sunday as the day of rest after the morning. We used to be up early and do the outdoor work in time to go to Sunday School and Chapel. Nothing done on Sundays but these basic needs. What a lot of difference it is today. They were hard times, but everybody seemed so different in those days. No doings to go to; but if there was any spare time, we used to go to a neighbour's farm and they come to ours and see each other's cattle for a little while of an evening and then go to bed early for getting up in time to start again next morning. What we had to look forward to was work; but, as I have said before, we were happier in those days. People were more contented.

In those days boys, when they left school in the country, went on a farm to apprentice and work. Their father used to agree with the farmer for them to stay there for twelve months. No doing as they pleased, and it was worth it too. And the girls had to do the same, just had a little time off one evening a week for a few shillings a week. And then very often Mother would collect it and give the girl just a little because the mother needed it to help keep the rest of the family. People tell about

11

what hard times it is now. It's nothing like it was then.

The men used to take a lot of pride in their horses. It was lovely to see a lovely pair of horses out in the fields working with their lovely brasses shining. The men were very proud of their team of horses. They all tried to have their horses looking well. Didn't matter what time they finished work as long as their work and their horses were looking well.

When I was young, the corn was all cut by hand with scythes. Then it was put in little lots and bound by hand. Then it was shocked; and when the grain was hard enough, it was carried to the farmyard and put in a stack until it was dry enough to go through the threshing machine.

Then it was hard work for us again indoors because we had to get food for a lot of men threshing days. And the farmhouses then all had stone floors to scrub and long kitchen tables to be scrubbed white - no table-cloths to cover them or mats on the floors. We had to black-lead stoves and shine them. I must say, a farmhouse kitchen always looked lovely. You could always see plenty of hams hung in the kitchen in bags.

The men wore hobnail boots, and they had to walk a long way to have their boots mended. In the evenings there was no concerts or pictures to go to, no half day off. Work was all we thought about, to get everything, cattle and crops, looking well. That was our pleasure.

There was another job that had to be done. All the farmyard manure the men had to load into carts and take out in the fields and put in little heaps. Then the men had to come with a manure fork and spread it all over the ground on the grass. Now they got an implement to drive to the door, and it's forked up, and it's taken right out in the field and scattered over the ground while the man is driving along on the muck-spreader.

Then after some years tractors came along, and things were not the same. And there wasn't the same interest took in things. And so it gradually got less interesting. Everything was done quicker. It was so nice in the evenings to look across the fields and see the corn and hay drying. But now everything is done so quick, there is not anything out in the fields to look at now. And before tea when you passed a farmyard there was a lovely herd of cows waiting to go in to be milked, but now not many people even milk a cow for their own use. Living in the country now is just like living in a town as far as cattle is concerned.

There is always something new to make it easier work, but still no contentment. But what I have said is my own experience of sixty years of life on a farm, and they were happy years.

Bessie Hicks Bate

BORN IN 1892, SPEAKING IN 1978

Sonia Watts' place was taken off of the Lugger for we when we came here to live. My father used to be under the Duke and Duchess of Marlborough, Blenheim estate, I suppose, one of the Royalty. And then we come down here. An' Gran took off they four rooms for us to go, separate from the Lugger. You can see a door in there in Sonia's bit that you can lead into the Lugger. And that was taken off for us when we come here to live. And then 'twas kept off, yu known, 'n' never put back again. Gran lived in the Lugger, you see.

Saturdays we used to do, well, anything we wanted to, really, Saturdays. That was our play day, di'n' us. We used to play on the quay. We wasn' chased off the quay as they are today. That quay was our playground. And nobody ever chased us off. We played hopscotch and lean up against the wall and jump on each other's backs 'n all sorts - I ferget what they call it.

There were four cottages there, as well, occupied by people. And there used to be three coal stores down there. And the boats used to come in and tie their ropes on posts. We had posts on the quay still. And they used to carry the coal across to they and put em in stores. Mr. Scott got his store; there was a coal store there. There was a coal store where doctors got their surgery, and there was a coal store where the Wharf is now. So we had three coal stores. We could play on the beach, but then, I mean to say, we used to play anywhere because there, you see, was no restrictions like there is today; you mustn't do this 'n you mustn't go there and you mustn't do this and you mustn't do that. They days is gone now. We could go 'n play where we like.

The quay, that's where they used to hang their nets. Mr. Pill an' they used to hang the nets, an' we used to swing in um. And then they had the crane there that they used to pull the stuff up with. This side they used to put the cargo boats an' carry the coal along that way. Oh yes, we used to swing in they nets, fine time. They never used to bother like that.

An the posts, we had three or four posts on the quay where they used to tie up the boats; one outside the Lugger An then there used to be the crane where they used to lift it all up in. Everything, everything was landed. A little ketch used to come in, an' bring it in from Plymouth.

The ferry boat was always a pullin' boat in they days. There was no motor boat. Mr. Walters brought the first motor boat here, an' he lined up with Hughie Evans. Cap'n Walters, he was the one that brought the motor boat here. But they used to pull across.

When we went over Fowey, we had penny return. If we got enough to get there, we used to go in the rowin' boat, when the tide was out. An' we used to go with the mens' dinners. They were workin' over Fowey, you know. We children used to take dinners. We used to stand there by where you go down the steps down to what's now Polmarine to see if the ferry was comin to Castle or to Polruan. Low tide we always went to Castle. You know, down through the Castle Ruins, down on the steps. That was where we used to go low tide. And then if it wasn't too low, we used to come into Polruan Quay and walk on a plank and land over Fowey Quay on a plank. When it was low tide we couldn't land at Whitehouse. You see, they lengthened the slip and lengthened the steps here, 'n you can go now any time. But back along, there wasn't that length of steps, you see. They brought 'em out.

We have been blown up the river in the ferry, and we've had to walk in from Carne Beach up to the fields many a time. Mr. Walters bought the ferryboat here. He bought the first motor boat here. We thought 'twas marvellous then, 'n so 'tis.

My grandmother owned the Lugger, you see. She and me two aunts, Aunt Rosie an Aunt Janie - that's Jimmy's mother and Mother's sister. An they runned it their selves. It belonged to the Hickses fer hundreds of years, yes. So, of course the aunts was still old, an' the War was on, 'n they couldn't run it. That's how it was sold.

Well, they used to come, open all day long, you see, they did, seven o'clock in the mornin's till eleven at night. No licensing hours in they days. And then on Monday mornings you always had a crowd of what they call Naval Reserve come down, from Polperro and Looe, with a haversack and a walkin' stick. They used to walk down, cuz of course, they couldn't afford - they di'n' have cars like they do today.

That big room - well it's all in one now, I think - well, that used to be Gran's parlour. Nobody was allowed in there, only Christmas time. We was allowed in there Christmas time when we used to go down to tea with her. All the grandchildren used to go down to tea with her, Christmas Day. And the bar, the place was open then. Well, you see, they've altered it now; they've made it into one big room. Well, it used to be - if you opened a latch door. The cellar used to be the one where they got the double door. Well, they used to keep all the cider there, barrels. An they used to have ther meals there when, yu know, when they was open because they di'n' have anybody in there then. An then we used to have our breakfast in the kitchen, where they sit now, public bar, like, yu know, one where you open door with a latch. That used to be kitchen. An' then we used to have our meals there in the mornin', breakfast always there in the mornin'. Where the gents' toilets is now - I presume - I never been in there - that used to be her larder place where she used to keep all her food 'n that.

An' up where you go to the stairs, Jimmy's mother had a shop there, a grocery shop. Jimmy Hicks, me cousin. His mother used to have a shop there, sold sweets 'n, well, every, yu know, grocery shop. Where you go up the stairs, wooden stairs? She used to have a shop there.

An' where Sonia Watts got her kitchen, that used to be the skittle alley where men used to go up 'n play skittles years ago. You can go in the pub an' go up the stair. They used to go, more or less, up the stair. Gran used to keep that door locked, cuz, you see, 'twas entrance to the pub, wa'n' it. You know, I mean to say, so you had to keep that locked. And then the toilet - there was a outside toilet up there, and Gran had an inside toilet for herself. I expect they're filling it up now, I dunno.

We used to go up skittle alley when 'twas wet weather. We used to go up there 'n play, yu know, out the wet. Yeah, we could have children in, yu know, we could have friends in to play. Gran didn't mind us havin' friends in to play as long as we didn't kick up too much noise, you know. We could go down under where Mrs Steele lives, we could go in that way. We needn't interfere with the pub at all, see, cuz there was age limit then for the pub, well, for children. An' we were all young, you see; so we had to go that way or else we couldn't go at all. 'Til we got of age, and then we went down the other way.

Then there used to be two or three shops on the quay. You could buy anything. There was more shops in the village than there is today, really, you know. Buy two penneth. 'Twasn't nothin. No elaborate shops.

And there was a tailor's shop on the quay, where Mrs. Hender used to be, a grocer's shop, a tailor shop, and a greengrocer's shop there. Well, there were three houses, separate houses there. Mr. Hender had it turned into one. Three separate houses, with a shop to each house. They lived at the back of them. Me aunt - she was called Roberts - lived in the middle one because, you know, he was a tailor, you know, made suits of clothes an all that. He was in the middle one an' the other was a greengrocer's shop and the other was a grocery shop.

Fore Street wasn't cobbles - only so far as Mr. Bedale's out East Street was cobbled over. They haven't long took em up, not all that long. Oh, God, you used to turn your ankles, my God, you know. 'Twas hard to walk on, admitted. But then you see 'twas what was in the place an' couldn't do no other. You know, you had nothin' else to walk with, really.

On the hill we used to have a bonfire before the council houses. I think they stopped the bonfire when they put the council houses up there. Up on the hill we always had our bonfire there. And they used to cut the furze down from the fields over there and up in the fields here, bring 'em down in barges, land it on the quay, an' used to drag it all up the street. Bonfires were for any special occasions, you know. Bonfire night we used to always have a bonfire on the hill. Now, we did have a bonfire then. Mountains high. We could see it go on burn for days.

And then the first of May they used to get a lot of tin kettles, a lot of old pots, buckets, and baths an that 'n drag around the streets. An' we used to have the policemen from John o' Groats to Lands End here to try an' stop 'em. They used to take 'em down Newquay an throw 'em in old ruins.

And then we used to decorate hoops. And the boys used to go out 'n get seagulls' eggs. And we used to blow them up and then raise all the seagulls' eggs on the hoops. We put one hoop and then the other hoop through - we had two hoops, really - I mean, it made four - and decorate it up with flowers, whatever we could get hold of. Pinch them off other peoples' gardens. Nobody never said nothin'. An we'd go aroun' singing "First of May is gardnin' day, and second of May is my birthday" and all this nonsense, yu know. Oh, we used to make our own fun. An' we used to have a good time. But now 'tis too much - mustn't do this, 'n you mustn't do that, 'n you mustn't go here, an' you can't go there. They days is gone.

We didn't have a lot of regattas 'n that here. That only come afterward, really. Used to have regattas up the river, Golant 'n Lerrin 'n all that. We used to go up there by boat, get stuck on the mud 'n all. The first one to get up to Lerryn used to get ten shillin'. When the tide was out. See, you had to go up to the tidal place - that's where it is today.

At Regatta time we used to go up, take the boat and go up to Lerryn or up to Golant. An' then, you see, the little train used to run to Golant years ago. We used to love to go up to Golant, walk up station an' catch the train an' see all the river goin' up. We used to go from Fowey Station up to Golant, pass all the jetties an' all that, yu know, as you went on. It was really a lovely trip. Then we used to go down to St Austell that way, see, from Fowey Station, always go down every so often, do our shoppin' St Austell. Used to go up 'n catch the train. It hasn't been shut down all they years.

Then at school we used to go what they call ramblin'. An' we used to have a teacher, Miss Taylor, who had a pony, an' she used to take us ramblin'. And the pony got lost. We used to go 'n look fer un. That was our ramble afternoon.

Then we had to work cause, you see, the wages wasn't much. And you had to do all sorts of things, you know. Some used to pick blackberries 'n' sell un, some pick water cress 'n' sell it. Because, you see, the wages were nothin' in they days. When they was workin' on the docks, they used to get eighteen shillings a week day work and a guinea night work. 'Twas well paid! Tuppence farthin' loaf of bread and a farthin' box of matches. Made it tuppence ha'penny.

We lived in the house over Mrs. Lamb got now - you know, next to Mr. Bartlett's up the steps. And I've stood out on they steps many times half-past eleven Monday mornin's - or Sunday night - to hear somebody comin' down fer Father to, you know, say "Old Mr Freed's comin' or Mr. so 'n so's comin'. Time to get a move. And they used to go up the docks then. Yeah, after Sunday was over, they go Monday mornin'. And that was in their night shift then. They start night work then. You see, they used to do a night shift and a day shift up there in the Docks in they days.

Our parents never went shoppin'. Always the children went shoppin'. There were shops here. This here where I'm livin' in now, this room was a shop and a livin' room. Where Audrey lives was the same. You could buy the whole lot fer a pound today, yu know. In they days a pound was, oh, a lot of money. Cuz, you see, men only used to get that fer workin' all night durin' the week.

There was a fish cannin' factory down here where Brazen Island is, where they used to can fish, pilchards. And all the old ladies used to sit on the quay with two great baths, one fer puttin' the rubbish in and one water fer washin' they. An' then they used to clean all the pilchards down on the quay 'n take un over to the cannin' factory.

An' they used to have a drillin' station here, you know. The Naval Reserve used to come down here to do their drill once a month. And they used to bring their own meals with un. They used to come from Mevagissey 'n Polperro, 'n Looe. Used to walk in 'n walk back again. They'd stay in here, lodge here, half-a-crown a week sleepin' accommodation. Well, they'd stay from Monday till Friday night, and then they'd go home again. That would be their half-a-crown a week, fer sleepin'.

We had threepenny hops up in the Battery. That's the Battery is over to Fowey, is the Armoury, is it now? That used to be out where Mrs. Egbert got her house. That's where we used to go. Piano, generally, you know. People would play the piano, you know, voluntary service, cause you couldn't pay nobody for that, really. You know, those who could play the piano used to play; an' those who didn't play used to do other things. Anybody went. 'Twas an evenin out wa'n it. You had cup of tea a penny, 'n a bun or a piece of cake or somethin' a penny. Always pennies; we had to work on ha'pennies 'n pennies in they days. We went all ages, you know. Girls at ten could go as well as girls at fifteen, you know. I mean to say, we all used to muck in together because, you see, you was glad for somebody to come.

Now, Mrs Grose, you know Mrs Grose. Well, her sister Winnie, she same age as me. Well, she's a good pianist. Well, she used to play the piano. It was voluntary, no expense to pay, yu know, like fer music nor nothin' cause they only had a piany, you see. And you did so much on the piano as you did fer the band, I reckon. Yu know, if you get somebody who can play. And, well, like she got tired somebody else jumped in. You know, I mean to say, it was all voluntary.

But today everybody wants to get paid for everything. If you sneeze, you gotta pay, nearly. 'Tis true. 'Tis true. But, no, years ago there was more good help, yu know. People would help one another.

A lot of men went to sea. They mostly did summer yachting, mostly. There was a lot of yachtin' down here. 'N then, the yard used to be in full swing. And down where Mr Toms got now, down there there used to be a blacksmith's shop. And then it used to be a yard as well.

There was plenty to do here, yu know. We never, we never without any job, yu know. Like entertainin' ourself. Cuz we had to make our own entertainment, and we used to do it. Concerts, used to do Band of Hope concerts. They were very nice, you know, do dialogues 'n singin' 'n recitin' 'n pay thruppence to go in. We had to go on coppers in they days not on pounds 'n shillin's 'n pence. Oh yeah, we always get 'um up ourselves.

We didn't mix with kids in Fowey cuz it was only a penny. But a penny was a lot of money in they days that you didn't go. You only, like, went over Regatta Day and different days like that, yu know, unless you went with dinner - the men was workin' or your father or your husband workin', an' you took dinner across to them, yu know.

Christmas we used have fun, used to dress up and go around what we called Darkey Partyin' in they days. Goin' around singin', dressed up, from door to door, knockin', get coppers, a penny from you, an ha'-penny from somebody else. 'Twas a small donation gratefully received. We'd sing anything, really, yeah. We went out around Christmas and like right up, used to go on right on till you welcome New Year in. and then you finished.

Then when they was turned out the pub, they used to come up corner and sing. Oh. it used to be lovely to hear em all singin', cuz they had lovely voices. Well. when Daphne was married, I think it was, Bobby and they were doin this singin'. And somebody complained. An' I think he was fined er somethin', and they never sang no more. Oh, used to have lovely singin' down there. Oh, the men could sing, yu know. Well, of course, there was Roy Tomlin - yu know the Tomlins - was there. They used to do that down the corner, down to quay after they turned out of the pub.

Cuz, I mean to say, I used to go to the Lugger a lot cuz my grandmother owned it, you see. And when they was turned out, Gran used to say, "Now be careful what you doin' out there. Going out 'n have a sing-song." An they used to go out there, an' it used to sound all over Polruan. Yeah, nobody said nothin'. We had a policeman here. Now you got nobody. We always had a policeman here. We used to hear the carol singers singing down this corner till one o'clock. Cuz our parents knew where we was to, you see. An you was only singin', an' half the parents used to come down too, you know, join in as well. An' besides, there was nothin to be afraid of here because everybody knew each other, you see. Wasn't like it is today, you know, so many strangers here. You'm lucky if you know your next door neighbour, really here now.

At Christmas always used to make their own cakes 'n put 'em by the fire--- to rise, to plum, they used to call it. And then if it didn't plum, 'twas heavy, and you couldn't eat it. Well, you could eat it, but 'twas hard. Yeast or barm they used to more or less use. Barm was somethin that they used to have it in a stone jar. Mrs Langmaid can tell you more about it than me cause her mother used to make it. You know, Phylis's mother-in-law. Her mother used to sell it. We used to go for a pound of barm when she lived in Elm Cottage, her mother. May Langmaid's mother, she used to make it and sell it. Well, there used to be two or three. Miss Curtis up the street used to sell it. And Mrs Chapman on the Quay.

In the house we decorated with paper decorations, 'n holly, 'n mistletoe, 'n all that sort of stuff. Everybody had a Christmas tree. My golly, we'd know if we didn't have a Christmas tree.

Dinners were always took to the baker to cook. Always. Well, we used to think that if they baked it, you weren't compelled to stay in to look after it, that's the truth of it. And you paid a penny to have it baked. Well, you couldn't bake it home fer a penny. The cakes, Christmas cakes, always was took to the baker. My, stacks 'n stacks, weeks before Christmas the cakes used to go down. Black cakes. He was givin' money for it, wa'n' he. An' his oven was empty. He didn' bake it when his was baked. He baked it when his was out or not made, you know. Always take it to the bakers, take yer pasty or your dinners to the bakers, penny to cook yer dinner. Well, you ain't goin to sit home on a stove 'n bake it. It was cooked lovely. We had three bakers here then - one where Beatie Thomas lives, one where Singin' Kettle is, an' one where it is today.

Mr. Millard had a shop there one time 'n sold bread, but no bake-house. Oh yes, he did - they had one underneath. Yeah, yes he did, but it didn't last very long. No, not long enough to remember, as they say. Yes, down under. Well, some strangers got the top part, used to be a dairy. That been all sorts, that little place has.

I think Mr. Libby was the first one to have a car in Polruan, and he come down to Penzance to pick me up, and I was the first passenger he had. That's Percy Libby's father. An' he was the first one to have a car. He had a dairy before; he had a farm. He used to drive us to Polperro. He didn't used to let it out. He would drive us in a - what 'e call a - I drove down there many a time with un - well, like a cart, open cart, you know, trap. Yeah.

This church was used more than she is now. She's hardly used at all, they tells me, now. Cuz you see, back in they days we had a vicar and a curate. See, so I mean to say, Mr Truscott used to live at the Vicarage an' Mr Walke lived in several houses here, the curate did.

We didn't have so much church out Lanteglos that you got now. Because we always had St Saviours. An' St. Saviours was always packed. Sunday night you had to go early to get a seat. You had to be there early else you wouldn't get a seat. People used to go to church an' children an' all lovely choirs, yu know, with cassocks an surplices, used to be. Oh yes, they had a lovely choir.

An' in where Pam, me daughter-in-law, lives used to be about eight or nine classes of children for Sunday School. That was our Sunday School when I was a kid. I see Bernard, me son, bought it twenty or thirty years ago. Oh we had hundred, two hundred children in that school. We used to be in classes with different teachers. You know, it was really an ordinary day school but a Sunday school. Very nice it was, you know. We went afternoons.

If it was Anniversary out Chapel, they used to have Anniversary an' they used to have platforms. An' they all used to sit on the platform, boys one side an' girls the other, of the pulpit. And they used to have Anniversary an' the choir up over, an' they used to have Anniversary teas out West Street, both Chapels.

Course it's all, it's too much trouble, I think, today. I mean, you haven't got the work, you see, scrubbin' 'n black-leadin', and, I mean to say, everything was done by hand wa'n' it? Now it is done with bloomin' Hoovers 'n God knows what all. That's the only thing that's done be hand. That's what I mean, 'tis a different day. And the cookin', you see, had to cook with black-leaded stoves. An' every Friday they used to black-lead their stove and clean their food out. Mrs. Steele does it now; 'n she's the only one, I think, got a black leaded stove. Wouldn't do away with un fer the world. She cooks all in that one. The other week I said, "Why ha'n' you took it out?"

She said, "May wants it taken out; I ain' gonna take un out." An' she cooks everythin' in it.

I said, "What do you clean it with, Ida?"

She says, Oh, can't get no black-lead now. Now I got boot polish to clean it." See, when the stoves went, the black-lead went. An' we used to put vinegar in it to soften it on a saucer or plate or somethin' an' to do it like that. You had brushes, you had one to put it on and one to take it off and another one to shine it with. She got all that out there.

Mr. Taylor converted Chapel Ruins out West Street into a house for hisself. It was the ruins of a chapel. Well, then it was sold to the Liberals to have a Liberal Club there. Well, then they couldn't raise the money to do the club; and he bought it as a ruins. Part of the walls left, not very high up, and then he bought it, and he converted it as well as he could. He didn't do a lot to it. Just so he could live there hisself.

Well, then he decided to go to Fowey cuz he was on the Council at Liskeard, y' know, he an' Mr Tippin', the schoolmaster. Mr Tippin' had the house down under. Well, then when he decided to sell it, he come to me an' he said, "I bought a house up Lostwithiel Street, and I got to sell Chapel Ruins to pay for the one in Lostwithiel Street." So he said, "If you don't buy it, no one else in Polruan will have it." An' I thought, well, me husband wasn't very keen on it because we lived in Miss Herberts's where Miss Herberts live. My husband never forgive me for shifting out there, you know. An he says, "What 'e want to buy that for?" But he wouldn't have nothin' to do with property ever. What I bought was my business. He wouldn't have nothin' to do with it.

So I thought it over, 'n my husband said, "You must be mad." But, then, I was always reckoned mad. So I bought it. An' course it was in my name. An' I paid 12/6 a week an' the interest on the money. I used to pay it in Lloyds Bank. An' that's how I bought me first house, an' I mortgaged that an' bought this. Well you see, there's a will if people was to purchase here years ago when property was so cheap. I bought the house where Mr Waterman used to live. I bought that one fer £50. An' that was sold fer, I forgot how many thousand Mrs Bigmead and Mrs Baker and somebody else sold it, didn' um? £50 I paid for that.

An' I bought the garages 'n all up Battery Park - that's all they eleven. I sold 'em to Mr. Mantin - you wouldn't know him, I don't suppose. He used to have the guesthouse where fish 'n chips shop is now.

After the fire I couldn't stay at Chapel Ruins. I didn't want to stay there after that cuz, I mean to say, that I lost everything; and that was that. My husband died in Chapel Ruins. And, well then, I sold it to Noles, that used to work for the boys years ago. And then I come over here an bought this lot, which is the better investment really. I mean you got lovely view here, and nothing can be built in front of you. These is old houses, yeah. Been here before my time, long before my time. Two hundred years old, I suppose.

The harbour was lovely in they days. It was never empty like this. No, see, they no such thing as pullin' boats up in they days. Cuz they had nowhere to put em. Cuz you see, this yard was occupied, 'n this yard was occupied. Doin' all. They was repairin' ships in Newquay Dock, you see. An', a course, rough weather, it was really a worry, wa'n it? Some broke away, they did. They do now, can't help it.

Mabel Mutton Broad
BORN IN 1897, SPEAKING IN 1983 AND 1986

Father was a Polruan man and lived in the little house opposite the chapel, Chy an For. He was an only child. His father died before he had trousers. He used to wear little skirts. He died of TB when he was thirty-one.

My mother was born at Herodsfoot. Her father, Thomas Stevens, worked in the powder mill and was killed in that. The stacks are still standing. He went to work one morning. My mother was a lady's maid, working where Graham's offices are for Mrs. Rogers (in Fowey, Fore St.). It was a private house then. She got the message her father was hurt, and ran from Bodinnick to Herodsfoot. He was dead when she arrived.

Gran Mutton was a lovely sewer, went around gentlemen's houses for a week sewing. She would be fed and get 10/-. She went out Pendower, took her little boy, went twice a year, spring and autumn.

My mother was married in 1881 on the 19th of February. And her first child was born on the 8th of December - that was Frances, my eldest sister. So she wasn't married twelve months before she had a baby. And she said she was so ignorant that she didn't know anything about married life or what it meant.

However, my father was working in Plymouth at the time. And it was when the King Street Chapel was being built in Plymouth. And he being a craftsman, as I told you before, he was one of the men that did part of the carving around the rostrum in King Street Chapel, which is still standing today.

Well, they lived there for quite a while. And they finished work, and they came back to Polruan to live. There wasn't very much work for my father, and times were rather bad. So he went in the sailing ships to Australia and all around the world. Father was a shipwright on sailing ships out to Australia etc. Mother got fifteen shillings a week. And by this time Mother had two more babies.

In Mother's day the Naval Reserve men trained at the Battery. One hundred and twenty came to do their month's training. Father was at sea. Mother lived where Quay House garage is now. She used to take in two Naval Reserve men from Mevagissey. They'd bring a quarter of tea or a tin of cocoa for evenings. Sometimes there were four men, paying a shilling each a week. They finished Friday nights, returned Monday morning. The men had the big bedroom with two beds. We children were all upstairs. There was a big kitchen down bottom at the back.

Father stopped home from sea, and he had an opportunity to go to Chatham Dockyard to work. So they packed up from Polruan, and they went to Chatham to live and had a very happy time. My mother loved it up there, really. And during the time she was up there, she had another baby son. So that meant that she had four children. They hadn't been there a great while before the depression started, and the Dockyard was sacking quite a lot of men. Well they didn't have very much money; so Mother decided that they couldn't afford to stay in Chatham waiting for the dockyard to re-open again.

So they came back to Polruan the second time. By this time she was living up at Newquay Cottages where I was born, and in the meantime she'd had two or three more children. So I was born up in Newquay Cottages in 1897, and we lived up there until 1906. And then the house was too small for us, and we came down to East Street to live where Mrs Newton has gone away from.

And we stayed there all our lifetime, which I called home, really, because I was only nine when we came down from the other house. And we lived there until Mother died, well, 1930, and I kept the house on for another twelve months. And then I went to Fowey to live with my sister because I couldn't afford to keep the house on.

As I told you before, we lived up in Newquay Cottages. And we had all these children, and there was only two bedrooms. I can always remember you had to go through one bedroom to get to the other because it was three-storey. And there was, 'course, Mother's bed for Mum and Dad. Dad was home from the sea by this time, workin' with Slades' people. With Mum and Dad was usually a cot by the side with the baby in and a cot the other side with the next one in. That was in that bedroom.

Well, up in the top bedroom we had three beds; one for the boys when they were youngsters, you see, growin up and one for the girls, cuz we were three girls. We all slept in two double beds, and the three of us slept in one bed. And then there was a cot because mother had an invalid son, and he used to sleep in the cot by himself. But there was plenty of room. We had a chest of drawers and like a wardrobe for all our clothes and everything. So we were quite happy up there.

When we were young we were sent to bed early of a summer's night; so mother could get her jobs done. We never minded. We'd sit at the window in our room and watch other children playing. Mother always spent two days a week washing - everything by hand and spotless white. She often couldn't start it till after tea. Whites one day, coloureds the next. In later years she had wooden rollers to wring out the clothes but not when we were children.

Mother had a hard life, really. She had rhumatoid arthritis after one child was born. She had thirteen children. Rhoda, when four, went to live with an aunt and uncle who were childless up country. Mother was probably about to have another baby. Rhoda wanted to go, never looked back. Two children, John and my youngest sister were not quite right - they never went to school. Today they could have gone to school.

Dr. Boger, a lovely man, doctor for years here, came one day. They were sitting in the window at a long table like they had then in the kitchen for dinner. He said to Mother, "You feed them too much, they won't live to grow up, you know."

Mother said, "They've got to eat, same as anyone."

My sister died when she was twelve. We took her up river one fine August day, went swimming with her brothers and sisters, such fun. She came back, had a cold, went to bed and was dead by September. I took her a mug of milk one afternoon, helped her out to a chair by the bed for her drink. She said," I don't know what's the matter!" and fell on the floor. We called the doctor. It was pneumonia.

I had four brothers. All had Eton suits with fairly big collars, which were washed normally, and ironed with a flat iron put on the stove in a shiny slipper to keep it clean. From that we went to the box iron you put hot coals in, getting red hot - a big improvement.

Ben Adams lived next to Mrs. Bigmead, up the steps (Betty Oons). He and his wife ran a mangle in the cellar under Mrs. Bigmead. Clothes were put in canvas which went between wooden rollers, then spread out when dry. Others who had mangles were Grannie Lean at Staggar Inn (West Street). We still ironed shirts etc. There was one on the quay years and years before.

Father worked as a carpenter for Slades for one sovereign per week. He'd bring it home and give it to Mother. She'd say, "Let me hold it a few minutes. Then I'll divide it out where it must go." Father had a shilling a week pocket money. A pint of beer cost tuppence. He didn't go down to the pub every night but always had two pints Saturday night. Every time Mother knew another baby was on the way, she'd put by thruppence a week in an egg cup. That was to pay the midwife who charged ten shillings.

Father worked evenings doing odd carpentry jobs. He always did what was needed at the Lugger, would fix a chair for someone, etc. He also helped his good friend, Johnny Stephens, to build boats (at Polmarine now). Mrs. Stephens, Johnny's wife, lived where Iris Heard does further along West St. She had a long table by the window, and she made all the sails for the ships, eyelets etc. Father could come home for tea, then lay down for half an hour, get up about six and go down to Johnny.

We had porridge always in the mornings. The stoves used to be lovely, shining. Friday afternoons I was allowed to stay home and black lead the stove. We always had velvet to rub it up with. There were two coconut mattings on top of the lino in the kitchen. Father used to make a navy blue rug in front of the fireplace, with J and M on it. Made rugs at sea - rag mats - from strips of Father's overcoat or someone's, coiled around a stair rod same as jute. We had a broad sofa in the kitchen. Mother was an invalid.

I want you to realize what a place Polruan was. The factory which is now Brazen Island was run by the Mevagissey Pilchard Exporters. Mr. Harvey came to Polruan as manager, and in the pilchard season boats would come in early in the morning, and women would be employed to clean and pack the fish. I believe as many as twenty people would be busily engaged. They had good wages for those days, about sixpence an hour, I think. You could also buy any surplus fish very cheap from the Quay, twenty or thirty for a shilling. These casks of fish would be loaded and sent to Italy, and even after our factory closed, the fish boats, you will recall, came to the jetties regularly and took cargoes to Italy and various other ports in the Mediterranean.

Newquay Yard always had a sailing vessel in dock, one usually in for the whole winter months for extensive repairs and in the summer smaller jobs. It was very unusual to see the dock empty. At the store by the dock was a well-stocked ships' chandler's shop. You could buy anything as they supplied all the sailing ships, and many of these would be going to be away many months to Newfoundland, Spain, and some to Australia and the Far East.

In East Street was one little grocery business run by Mrs. Mitchell where Mrs. Bate now lives. Her living room was divided by a wooden partition; the shop as you entered and the living-room inside. You could get almost anything there - paraffin which they kept down in the cellar. I can remember the stairs always creaked when Miss Mitchell went down to measure out the oil.

At the corner you will all remember Mr. John Salt and his wife. They had a shop full of everything - newspapers and tobacco and sweets - where the Sea Chest is now. He was also Insurance Collector and Rate Collector and Town Crier.

Down to the Quay. Slade's Yard was a very busy one run by Mr. Slade and then his three sons, employing forty or fifty men. A very busy coal store run by Captain Stone, previously by his father. And several times a year the sailing vessel

25

was in discharging her full cargo of coal, which we could buy for about two shillings a hundredweight, and it was delivered in the little pony and cart. The other coal store was first where the Rescue Shop is now (Doctors' Surgery) and was run by Captain John Bate Slade, who also kept the Russell Inn. Later he shifted to where the Lugger store and garage is. His coal was delivered by donkey, the bag of coal slung over the donkey's back, and Mr. Welsh, 'Stroppy' as we used to call him, would walk the donkey up and down over steps all over the village. He was also the Chimney sweep and a general handyman.

There were three shops on the Quay. There was dear old Mrs. Chapman in the first house, before Mrs. Hender had it all turned into her guesthouse. At Mrs. Chapman's you could buy all sorts, her speciality being marinated pilchards and mackerel. You could buy as little as threepence worth, and in the winter it would make a lovely savoury tea. Also pickles - she would have the big seven pound glass jars, and you could buy tuppence or threepence worth of those.

Next was a nice draper's shop. Previous to my memory I believe a tailor's shop run by Mr. Skinner. And when it became the drapery, Miss M. Johns, who later became Sister Hocken's mother, ran it. I always remember the lovely polished counter and the nice materials you could buy there.

In the house inside was Mrs. Roberts, who was a kind of newsagent. We always went on Saturday afternoons for our papers; the Christian Globe for Mother, Tit Bits and Pearson's Weekly for the boys, and the Western Weekly for Dad. And we had to buy a quarter or half pound of tea to help Mrs. Roberts out, as she was the agent for that as well.

Then the Lugger Inn, which was run for so many years by the two Miss Hickses, previous to them, their parents. I remember the old lady with her curls and a lace cap, a real Victorian. Then the Mangle House where old Mrs. Bate lived, and where we took our clothes to be mangled in the old-fashioned wood box mangle.

Then out to where the Winklepicker is now, a wonderful sweet shop then run by Mrs. Thomas; homemade rock - I believe three sticks for a penny -, toffee apples, winkles, cockles. She really was a character.

We then had the sailmaker's loft run by Mr. Barrett. And then the fishermen's nets all being repaired and dried on the Quay. I expect most of you will remember seeing them all hanging on the big wood rafters that went from the linney to the end of the Quay where there was a crane used for discharging goods which were brought by boats from Plymouth - groceries for the shops, etc - as nothing came by road in those days.

At the Corner Shop Mr. Taylor, 'Georgie' as everyone called him, his wife, a lovely woman with beautiful golden hair, and daughter. The shop was full of muddle but stocked everything. Chemistry as well, in fact all the cures for all ailments. A devout Church man, I believe, a Church Warden. And he also had the baker's shop where the Co-op was.

Then next to the Russell was Mr. Clogg's - cream, eggs, veg, and meat. A wonderful family - they all went to Canada in the early 1900's before the First World War. Then the Reading Room as it still is and the other side of Garrett Steps was a nice shop, haberdashery, owned by Mrs. Blamey with wool, nice materials, lace, cottons etc. Then out to the two mangle houses. Ben Adams and Granny Lean, all with their regular customers, which helped to eke out the little bit of money they earned.

Down over the steps where Mrs. Tomlin now lives was a dressmaker's work room which Miss Buley ran. She usually had two working for her and was always full of work. Then out to Miss Dyer's dressmaking house where Mrs. Byles lives now. She employed several apprentices. I think Mrs. Steele and poor Mrs. Laiety learned out there.

Then where Lodsworth is now was the post-office and grocer's shop run by Mr. Charlie Stephens and his mother. They had best quality goods. One always had to pay a few coppers more at his shop.

Then, of course, we must not forget the Pills with the crab and lobster trade, also salmon seining. It was a sight to see them shooting the nets off the Castle and sometimes just off the Quay and seeing the lovely silver salmon being landed. I have seen them land four or six at a haul. Where has it all gone? My husband was in the goods yard for years at the station, and the Pills and Uncle Bill Climo would bring up their crab and lobsters in the proper containers to catch the four o'clock train out from Fowey for the fish to be in London at Billingsgate Market for the morning sale.

And now into Fore Street. Next to the Corner Shop, where Bartlett (No. 2) is now, was a barber shop, a Mr. Craney and his son, there for years. And the baker's shop was taken over by Mr. J. Hender of Fowey.

Then the Sunray (No.9). That was a thriving shoe repairer's and shoe shop run by Mr. Shepherd, an old gentleman, who, when he retired, brought Mr. Goldsworthy to Polruan to carry on the same kind of business and later to have the post-office as well.

Then Mr. Parsons, baker, a bake-house where everyone took their dinners etc. to be cooked, and at Christmas time borrowed his tins to make all the saffron cakes in, and what a number! Dozens of cakes baked. And his shop would be full on a Saturday evening, everybody buying sweets for Sunday, all those tins of Rowntrees Gums - can you see them? Also the tins of different kinds of toffee all cracked up along the counter, a really thriving shop.

Then the butchers. Mr. Holton is as far back as I can remember. Also when he brought his bride from Polperro and Mrs. Holton was in the desk in the shop. We would be sent on Tuesday and Thursday for the meat before going to school, with your own plate - sixpence a plate full of liver, skirting, etc.

Opposite was Mrs. Bunny's lovely shop - homemade brawns, cooked ham, fresh veg, lettuce, chipples, etc, and fresh buns and scones etc. Next to her, Mrs.

Menear. A real dear family. Mr. Menear the dustman, and the shop, potatoes, turnips, etc, but not very business-like, I think.

Then where the Co-op is. Two memories first. A drapers shop - I think Grannie Welsh ran it. But after her, a better memory of Mrs. Libby, with the dairy - lovely pans of milk and cream, eggs, etc. And they were there quite a while. Then later it became Mr. Cossentine, and what a shop he had, everything for this time of year, Spring Cleaning. Paper from threepence a roll and six pennyworth of oak or mahogany stain to do up all the kitchen chairs and tables. And we were quite happy with it all. No Formica tops etc. then, just plain white scrubbed tables in everybody's homes.

I must rush on to where Penhallow is now. That was another shop full of everything - groceries, china, pots and pans, run by Miss Puckey and her sister who later became Mrs. Roberts and Mrs. Grundy. What a business they had, and one would always have a good laugh if you went in there. They had a real sense of humour.

Then to Mrs. Edie Thomas's house, another bake-house, run by, I think, a Mr. Grant with a few groceries in the front room. Then, in the court to Mr. Drew's barber shop, tuppence for a shave, and always a shop full in the evenings. He was also Insurance Agent, and a Club Agent. Opposite next to Mrs. Miller's, Miss Godfrey had yet another grocery stores.

Then on to where the post-office is now, a real hive of industry. Shoe repair, boots and shoes for sale, china and wallpaper their chief items, but you could get all sorts there. Mr. Simmons, Nigel's grandfather, and his brother Tom would work until ten or eleven o'clock on a Saturday night, and Mr. Simmons was a great man for talking about politics. And you always knew he had an audience on Saturday - a few young chaps who would go to collect their repairs, etc.

Then, into Mrs. Glanville's, a really nice grocery, and as we know, Mrs. Congdon has not really given up so very long. Next door to her Mrs. Green, who, I think, sold homemade bread and barm (a leaven) we bought for making our own bread and cake. Then on to Mrs. Curtis and Bessie (Mrs. Palmer's house). She also sold barm and apples. Do you remember going in for a pennyworth on our way to school, always going in around the back to pick up one or two windfalls extra? And they were lovely little sweet eating ones.

I haven't mentioned all the places you could buy milk - Mr. Laiety's next to us, Mr. Thomas up Chapel Lane, Mr. Crapp up at the top where Mr. Hamilton Pearce lives now. And Mr. Abbott, who had a shop at Tinker's hill with sweets and groceries.

We also had several carts laden with greengroceries which came once or twice a week. Mrs. Rollings from Pelynt, Mr. Crapp from Cliff who came down river in the boat with lovely plums and apples. No scales to weigh them, so the plums would be sold by the hundred, and it was a work of art to see her counting them out, ten in each hand at one time.

Father Walke lived over the Corner Shop, then owned by Varcoes. There was hymn singing down on the corner; parson there, boys with candles on Sundays - sometimes an evangelist, 'Happy Dick'. Another, Martha, went up in the pulpit with him, her brother in law - Mrs. Bray's father, a lovely preacher. My father would go there when he was there, also if Tommy Marks was preaching. We used to have lovely preachers, such as Jolliffe.

Chapel and Church were very separate. Both chapels used to be full up. There was a choir full of men Sunday evenings. We children would go to a short Sunday School from ten till eleven Sunday morning, then Chapel service eleven till twelve, then home to dinner, back to Sunday school from two till three in the afternoon, then up on the hill to play, boys and girls, till tea. Then the men would gather about half five at the corner to sing hymns before going to Chapel at six again. When we were little we didn't go to evening chapel; but when we were about five and we could behave, then we went.

Sometimes a man with an organ would come to the village and play hymns at the corner where the telephone kiosk is now, where the pump was years ago. This was his Sunday Evening contribution, and mothers with young babies in prams who couldn't go to Chapel would gather and listen. People took it very seriously then, the opposite extreme from today.

Each Chapel had its Anniversary. It was always a full chapel both places. The one down the street here would be Whit Sunday. And the one out at the Wesleyan would be later in the year, June or July. But always Whit Sunday would be down at the small Chapel down here. There were two platforms, one each side of the rostrum - the men would go down and make that on the Saturday. And there'd be boys packed one side and girls the other, and both choirs all full of men singin'. We'd be practicin' for weeks before, like, couple or three times a week, the special hymns that we were going to sing. And everybody had new clothes - everybody had new clothes to wear for those special occasions. I don't know where the money came from, but they did.

And then, on the Monday we would go around singing the same hymns or songs to everybody that was sick in the village and finish up with a huge tea spread out in the Sunday School for children and grown-ups. There was always plenty to eat. Everyone brought something; certain women were designated to cut the cakes etc.

Or, on special occasions, we would have wagons, you know, that they used to bring the hay and that in when they were collecting that. We would have the wagon to take us to a field if the weather was nice, lent by a farmer, and have our tea party out there. Which was lovely, and boys and girls all together. Sunday School Tea Whit Monday. The food left was used for the Choir Outing on Wednesday. For this the prime motor-boat towed six or seven boats behind. All were welcome, not just the choir. Anyone who could get about would go. Mr. Roberts came down Moville to present prizes. So we used to have a really wonderful time and enjoy it. That was one of the special days.

And then there was Band of Hope. We always used to have a Band of Hope service as well. Sign the pledge when we were all about nine or ten out the Sunday School. Everybody signed a pledge, but we always had to sign a pledge. And there was a lovely lady used to run it. I think there was two. One of them went abroad, called Miss Madson. And the other one married Mr. Kempler after. And she was called Miss Reeves, I think, before. And they were very very good Christians really.

There was a magic lantern. Sam Buley ran it. Pictures of donkeys and drunks falling off and a motto what you should do. Children would be singing "We'll turn our Glasses Upside Down" and

"My drink is water bright, water bright
 My drink is water bright, from the crystal spray."

Granfer Dunn (Moses, with a beard) told stories of drunken sailors. He'd be at a rickety table in the Sunday School, and he'd wipe his eyes as he told us the sailors would drown. There was awful green ribbon weed on the water in the harbour at that time. After dredging that disappeared. And that was another evening that we had, you see.

I remember Mother hadn't had the children baptised. There was a vicar and a curate here then. Archie was fourteen or fifteen then; so they wouldn't baptise him though he wanted to be. He came home disgusted. "I won't go to Church. I'll be out Wesleyan Chapel!"

The restoration of Lanteglos Church was about 1906 when Edgar was born. Mother wanted him to be christened. They went up in a boat to Pont. He was the first of two to be baptised after the Restoration, baptised by Rev. Trusted.

We weren't dull. Besides, the church had the threepenny hop, that I expect you've heard about, down in the Church Sunday school, well, where Pamela lives now (The Old Schoolhouse, by the Village Hall now). That was the Church Hall in those days. And they used to have a threepenny hop once a week. Which, you see, we weren't dull. It was only a piano, but still it was quite nice. And it used to keep the children all together. Which was something for them to look forward to, wasn't it? You see, there's nothin' - well, of course, there's the Cubs and the Guides and that. But there's nothin' very much to entertain the children, is there, today?

We used to entertain ourselves, yes. We used to do all kinds of things out there. And then we used to have concerts as well, you know, out there. Concerts at any time - to make a bit of money. Both Sunday Schools had platforms and curtains, not just the school. Hanging oil lamps were the only light. The village all came - it was full - steaming in wet weather. And little plays, you know, they used to get up for the Chapel or the Church. Used to have lovely times, really. There was always somethin', sort of, you could go to, you know, say from six to seven or six to eight if you were a bit older. And it weren't dull. You didn't have to stay in every night wondering what you could do. Always somethin' to do.

Pubs were men's things. Women used to go with their jugs for beer dinner time. If a lady went out to meet another man all dressed up like a poppet, we used to think it awful in those days.

And then, of course, most of the young men used to belong to the Readin' Room, which is still there now. My brother used to go down there down below. He was a great reading room fan. He always went down there nearly every night. My brother always said he was on the water wagon, the one who lives in Canada. He never drank or smoked in his life. He would go to Reading Room, come home at nine o'clock. You could time him, that one. You would get the kettle on - cocoa it used to be in those days. Nine o'clock the knob of the door would go, an' in he would be comin'. You could time him. See, they had to be up early in the mornin' to go to work. An' by the time they had their supper an' got to bed, it used to be ten.

Mother worked hard. She never stopped. But Dad was good, because Sunday mornings he'd get up, seven o'clock, and bring tea to all the family, all we kids - we all had our tea brought to bed and a biscuit. That was first thing. Then he used to go down and do the vegetables, always did the vegetables before any of us were allowed down. And, well you know, there would be a great big enamel pan of potatoes, and then there would be turnips, you see, for all the crowd. And that would all be done. And then perhaps by that time it would be gettin' on for eight o'clock before Mother was out. He used to say, "I'm just going up around the hill, Mother..."

May Day. Girls made garlands of flowers in the morning. There were some beautiful ones. One or two always stood out. Sometimes a girl would blow out some eggs and decorate the shells for the front of the garland. The girls would all wear their best clothes and wear the flower garlands. Some were hoops, some crosses, and a band around the head. We paraded, three or four on our own anywhere, joined up, called on people, showed our decorations, sang songs to the sick. Then at school we would have a maypole and have dancing round the maypole. Everyone in the village used to come up to see.

The boys saved tin cans which they put down the Bound, collected them, tied them up with string or rope. Then May Day morning they would go through with the tin kettles and cans. Sometimes the girls joined in. The end of this (custom) was when a ship's tank was used. It ploughed the street up. The policeman was lifted on to the top of the tank. Bulls horns were blown, a deep tone.

Christmas was lovely. We'd have a tree with coloured balls. Father would say, "I've seen our tree out in the field." Then, when the time came, he'd bring it in. We didn't ask much. Father was handy, being a carpenter, and would make a wheelbarrow for one, a small kennel for a toy dog for another. I had a doll's house once. Mr. Widlake's daughter was a little older than me, and once I had a doll and cradle she was finished with. I would sit for hours rocking it with my foot and doing French knitting - you know, with four nails in a spool to make a little rug to go beside the cradle.

Father made a horse for Edgar in the kitchen to play with the Holton boy. The two would sit on the sofa 'driving horse', 'come fly'. Mother didn't mind who came in the house to play. Helen said it was the same up at Ferry Climb. They played

31

football on the lovely lawn until there was no grass left. The ball would land in the cucumber frame outside the kitchen door. Dad was irate. Mother said "We have to let them play. You don't want not to know where they are."

They used to dump ashes into Lady Ram's cove by Furze Park. Archie used to go out there and catch birds, kept stopping away. Father warned him, then belted him upstairs. We were all crying down in the kitchen, Will, Mother, and me. Mother was afraid we would fall over the cliffs. Several were lost over the cliffs. One Hicks boy fell over the cliffs. Crapp's horse leapt over, cart and all.

While Mother was alive my brother, that I told you, went to Canada. He always sent her the rent; so she had nothing to worry about. The rent was £9 a year when he went there to live, and he used to send her £3 every quarter to the post-office out at Charlie Stephens out at West Street. And you had to go out there to change it, the postal order. And the rent was £2.5/- a quarter, and the other paid the rates. So she had no worry about the rent or rates of the house. And he continued paying that till my mother died, which was from 1906 to 1930. Which was a marvellous son to do it.

Well, eventually, my father died in 1922. And there was no widow's pension nor anything. So if my brothers had not been good to my mother, we would have been like all the rest. We'd have been on the Parish. Because there was only me which was working, getting about a pound a week over in the grocer's shop in Fowey. And my youngest brother went to sea as an apprentice with the Hayne Company of St Ives. He passed his Captain's ticket, you see, and went on the British tenders afterwards, until the war. But there was nothing then from 1922 till 1930 that Mother had of her own money. So she was dependent on what I brought home from the shop and what the boys sent her. Cuz you couldn't save any money with a family like we had.

Well, when she was seventy in September she was like a person that was going to have £100 a week, to get 10/ a week from the post-office at seventy. Just to have 10/ a week of her own money to buy a pair of stockings or a little fancy scarf like they used to wear.

And eventually my brothers started to go away. First of all, my eldest brother went and served his apprenticeship with Mr. Renton down at the blacksmith's shop, down behind Newquay, where Mr Toms is building those new houses in the yard. He left school at fourteen and he had to serve seven years, a shilling a week to start with, and it increased a shilling each year until he was twenty-one. And Mr. Renton, the blacksmith, was a good craftsman, taught them well. And he had three apprentices. There would be a senior and then another one second, and he then he would take a junior one on when he left school. So he always had three boys working for him as well. Because, of course, there was all the ironwork for the ships and also all the ironwork for the horses. You see, they used to make the horse shoes, They used to make all those kind of things down there and anything else in the iron way would be made down there. He was a marvellous craftsmen, really, and brought these boys on very, very well.

Well, after me brother served his apprenticeship, there was no work in England; and of course he went abroad to Canada. Well, first of all, he went to America; and he didn't like it very well. And he was out there when Wall Street collapsed. So he stayed as long as he could; and then he thought, "Well, there's no work out here. So while I got the money to come back to England, I better go home." So he came home and did a few odd jobs here where he could get them and then eventually went to Canada again, the same year as the Titanic went down.

Well then, my next brother - the one next to him, that was drowned at forty-six, he started as apprentice at Slade's Yard when he was fourteen. First year, of course, they ran errands; took tools across to be sharpened etc. One day old Mr. Slade said, "What you doing, boy?"

"Taking this to be sharpened," he answered.

"You seem to spend all your time taking tools to be sharpened!"

At that the boy got angry and said "Sharpen it yourself!" and walked out.

Next day Old Mr. Slade came to mother and asked what was wrong, said he never meant anything. But Mother said, "You scolded him. He'll never go back. He's made up his mind to go to sea."

A man in Polruan had a ship in London, one man short in the crew and said to send the boy up there by train. Mother was nervous because he had never gone further than Par, perhaps. The man said not to worry, to give the boy a change of clothing in a sailor's bag (blue kerchief bag), and that someone would meet him at Paddington to get to the ship. The ship was coming to Polruan next anyhow. She did, and when he arrived with the ship, he was so keen. The crew said he was a born sailor. Whenever a sail had to be furled etc, he was up in the rigging like a cat. He went as a sailor from here, really, on the Hockens boats, the sailing ships that used to go to Australia. And of course he met an Australian girl and got married and stayed out there.

And then, my next brother was a plumber. He was five years older than me. So he went, when he was fourteen, over to to work at Mr. Lovering's to serve his apprenticeship with him as a plumber and gas fitter. And the shop was where the electric light shop (Bartletts, Fowey) is now; that was the plumber's shop. And they had the workshop down at the back that used to come out on the quay. I think it's all closed up now. I'm not quite sure, but I think it's all closed up now. But that's where they used to do their work down there. And he was marvellous, really. He served six years over there. And he was twenty in the June, and he left for Australia in the October. My sailor brother that was out there wrote home and said there was plenty of work in Australia; and if there was none in England and he liked to out there, he would send the £10 fare for him to emigrate out. And he went out there, and of course he never came home from there.

And then, my next brother, he was more or less a little bit delicate when he was young, didn't go to school very much because he had chest trouble and they were always afraid he was going to develop TB. He was always happy up on the farm up on the top with one of the farmers up there; whoever had the farms up there he would be up there. And then eventually, he went with Mr. Holton to start off with, that's Dick's father. And they used to go up in a wagon to Lostwithiel to the cattle market there on Mondays. And he would buy the cattle, and they would be brought home. And my brother used to have to walk behind with Mr. Holton going on ahead in the wagon, walk all the way from Lostwithiel to keep the cattle on the road that he was bringin' home; so it didn't wander back.

Well then, of course, the next day 'twould be killing day, and in the place what Dick's got now for his garage that was the killing house. They used to kill their own cattle out there on the Tuesday. Usually on the Tuesday morning the cattle would be killed . Of course, that was lovely. They was thrilled to bits with that. My brother used to be thrilled to bits with that, enjoyin' himself up there.

Well eventually, he was getting too old, then, to stay up there with Mr. Holton. And he went to Fowey, then, to Liddecoats to finish his apprenticeship where Kittows Butcher's shop is today. Then the First World War came, and he was in Bodmin, then, working for Eastmans after.

Well, of course, everybody was joining up then. Kitchener's Army, you know, a shilling a week it was, I think, yes, I think it was a shilling a week they had. You know, there was a poster up "Kitchener Wants You", "The Army Wants You". So lots of these boys joined up, and they went off to France. I think they had a terrible time, a really terrible time over there.

However, they came home. He was with the DCLI's. And they had a marvellous do in Fowey for them when all the Territorials and all the DCLI boys came home. And I always remember a speech was made by one of the army captains up outside the Safe Harbour, as it is now. And the place was packed with people up there. And of course they were praising up the Territorials, really, because there was such a lot of local boys in that. And my brother shouted out, "What about the DCLI?" That was the Duke of Cornwall's. So of course he brought that into his speech, as well then afterwards, because there wasn't so many in that regiment locally, here.

Well, we had a marvellous time. And everybody was dancin' through the streets and enjoyin' it, you know, celebrating just like they do now after a war and everything. Well, that was that.

Well, he came home not 100 per cent in health, and he was under the doctor. Well, he didn't know quite what to do. So, it was Dr. Boger in those days. And we'd been writing out to Australia to my other brother. And he wrote home and he said if Will would like to come out to him, he was sure that the climate would do him good. Well, we got in touch with the local person at Fowey that used to do the travel agency, like they do now, and he put us on the right road to get there. And my brother went to Australia not very well. Dr. Boger said, "Well," he said, "I'm really putting down a lie on the paper." You see, they wouldn't accept them unless they were fit. So he said, "I'm really putting down a lie but," he said, "it will extend his life five years if it doesn't any more." So he thought 'twas worth the risk of going.

However, he went and sailed from Southampton. My sister was in London at the time. And she went down to Southampton to see him off. And she said never again would she go to see anybody off on a ship because the ship was packed with emigrants going out, and she said all she could see was just his white face. You only look for your own, don't you? All she could see was his white face, and she said she thought "Oh dear, I'm never going to see him again."

So he went, and of course it was all sea trip in those days. And they went around Capetown, South Africa - didn't go through the Suez, I don't know for what reason - but, however, they went down Capetown way. And by the time he got to South Africa, he was better, his cough and everything. He was a like a new man.

And by the time he got to Australia, he never looked back in his health. He lived to be over seventy, and worked hard. We used to send out the local newspapers sometimes.

When my brother came home he wasn't really a Christian, you can understand. But if I was goin' around the house and somethin' come up, he could always quote something from the Bible. So I said to him one day - he came home in 1952 the first time - I said, "How do you know so much about the Bible? Cause," I said, "You don't profess to be a Christian."

So he said, "I'll just tell you the reason," he said. "When I went to Australia, you know what Mum was like." Course, she had to give him the Bible. "And there was nothing else to read, only the papers that used to come out from home and, of course, the letters. But there was no papers delivered. There was no daily papers or anything up the country. So I used to read the Bible." And he said, " I won't say I read it once; I read it many times," and he said, "That was how I know the quotations from the Bible."

So, that was me brothers. Well then, of course, when the youngest one come on, well, we always say he had the best end of the stick because, you see, the others were all grown up and gone. And then he went to sea. That's the one that's living now that lives in Weymouth.

However, my sisters. The eldest one, as I told you, was a dressmaker, served her apprenticeship over at Rowes where Midland Bank is now. That was a big shop, quite a business, with a dressmaker's room, a milliner's room, and also a department selling linos and carpets, in which they employed boys and men to look after that department. And, of course, several were behind the counter.

And on a Saturday night it was quite a busy place, Fowey, for shoppin' because men weren't paid, you see, until about four o'clock on a Saturday. They worked until four o'clock. So the men weren't paid. Therefore, everybody went to Fowey Saturday evenings from six to eight - shops kept open until eight or nine o'clock - and did their shoppin' then. And outside of this draper's shop, they used to put a counter out Saturday evenin's; and you'd have all the remnants and different things that you could buy on this stall outside. And it was quite a business in Fowey in those days, and everybody go and do their shoppin'. Grocers' shops keep open, 'n, well all shops, up to eight o'clock.

Butchers, then you'd get the odd bits, you know. Cuz there were no fridges or anything, you see. They had to get rid of it. All fresh you see. You couldn't have - no fridges or anything to keep it in in those days. And summer time it wouldn't keep. So, you see, you'd get bargains Saturday evenings. Lovely shin - you would buy the whole leg of shin for four pence a pound. We always used to have one of those. Mother always used to have one of those because, with my brother working in butcher's shop, perhaps it would be sixpence a pound. Well, I say the money wasn't much; but it went a long way because you could get things so cheap, you see.

On Thursday you could buy sixpence worth of bits - liver, beef, scrap ends of steak etc. from Holton's - that would be over roast (pot roast). Mrs. Holton had a lovely face, dark hair, in a white overall. She would take money in at the desk (in 1906), helped her husband, worked with him always.

Well, my older sister worked as an apprentice, as I told you, at dressmaking. And after that she kept on as a dressmaker and stayed on there for years. She was made head skirt hand. They used to make suits, you see, in those days. Well, there would be one that would be better for coats and another one better for skirts. Well, my sister was skirt hand and blouses.

Well, I don't know whether you've heard their name; but Quiller-Couch's wife and the people that kept Tredudwell, which was called Allchin in those days. Well, they could come in and give orders, you know, for their street clothes that they should be made to fit. And they would have blouses made, silk in summer and warmer vyella ones in winter. Really good quality ones with tucks all down the front, you know, and they had quite a business.

When the sales came, my sister would take her wages out in materials to bring home, for she made all our clothes; flannelette for father's shirts which were lined because he was a little chesty, black for my blacksmith brother so they wouldn't show the dirt, cotton for my plumber/gas fitter brother because he was prone to be sweaty, and prints for us. I liked blues and greens and pale lilacs, any floral.

When someone died all went into deep mourning. My sister would sit up all night making a costume etc. for the funeral.

Besides, there was millinery, all hats. And the fun the girls used to have tryin' on all these new hats when they came in, you know, unknown to the head one, the older one, you see. But they really had a lovely time. We liked white straw hats, the ones with the longest streamers was always the smartest.

And nobody took any notice of crossin' the ferry, which was only just a rowin' boat. They used to row boats, row 'em over in those days and didn't take any notice of it. And in the winter time when it was very stormy, you had to cross over at Bodinnick and walk around from Bodinnick to Polruan to get home in the evenin's. And my father many a time has come out on the road and not only him but other people's dads as well would come out to meet us on the road to see that we were comin' home safely with a lantern with a candle in, you know, to light us on the way to get home. And like the storms that we do get here now, we got them just as bad then in those days. And then, that was how we used to get home. Sometime it would be two and three times a week we'd have to walk home from Bodinnick to get home from work. Didn't take any notice of it. Wasn't easy. None of it was easy in those days, but we managed.

Well, then, my other sister, I told you, was adopted by my auntie. And she went to Cumberland which was then, Cumbria now, of course. And she was brought up with my auntie, and she lived there all her life. Course she used to come home to see us sometimes. But she never wanted to come home to live. Cuz Auntie never had any children, and Mother had nine.

Well, then, my next sister she went as a nannie. She was fond of children; and she went first of all, I'm not quite sure how she got to know those people, but she worked first up with the Rev Walke up there just helping out when he lived up where Mrs. Pearce is livin'. And I think it was people up there staying that said they were goin' on holiday, and they wanted a nannie, an under-nannie. There was a head nurse, and then she went as a under-nanny with this family. And they trained her, and so she continued right up until she was married in 1917.

Well, then, I was rather unfortunate, really, because, you see, being the youngest home, mother was more or less an invalid after my youngest brother was born. I was nine when he was born. She must have been between forty-six and forty-seven when she had him, and she really had a bad time. And she developed rheumatoid arthritis, and she couldn't do a thing. So, therefore, I was only a schoolgirl; but I still had to do a lot of work home besides.

And when I was thirteen, I was allowed to stay at home in the mornings to cook the dinner and that and go to school in the afternoons. So that was how I never learned percentages and all that because it was just the year I would have been learnin' that. I was good at arithmetic, but I never learnt that at all, you see, I missed all of that. I used to go in the afternoons. When I was thirteen and a half, they let me off of school altogether; so I could stay home and look after mother and the rest of the family, you see. And then I stayed home because she was an invalid, and I stayed home then until I was twenty-one.

Well, there was a doctor in Fowey called Dr. Tabb, and he had rheumatoid arthritis as well. And he used to walk with two sticks. And one day Mother said to him, "Isn't there anything, Doctor, you can give me?"

"Well," he said, "I can't cure you. I shouldn't be walkin' around like this if there was a cure. But," he said, "I can give you relief." So he used to give her pain killers. And after a certain period the pain went although she was crippled, you know, one hand was like that. But still she was better because she wasn't in any pain. But she'd suffered all the pain for about six or seven years, I think it was.

However, time went on, and by this time the family had grown away, and they were all gone. I said to Mother, I said, "Well, I think, really, I could do with a job and still look after the home in between times." If she could manage and sort of get the meals, you know.

And I went and got a job over in the grocer's shop in Fowey where the Dewhurst is (Delicatessen now) but was the Star Tea company in those days before it became International. Well, we really had a wonderful time over there, and I worked there for eighteen years, I think. I started at about five shillings a week, and when I finished after eighteen years, I was getting the large sum of sixpence less than thirty shillings a week. So that was how we got paid.

Work in a shop then was different altogether. It was work in those days, not just standing behind the counter serving. We had a rota every day that we had to do so much in between the serving time. I mean, you were still serving. I was on the grocery department. There was two 'fellas' on the provision side. It was a marvellous shop in those days, a marvellous shop. We sold everything. And the stock, it all used to come down from London by rail in great big cases. And then they had a lorry used to bring it down from the station. It would be all unpacked in the store by the side.

And the bacon that we used to sell, great sides of bacon would come in. We'd have about ten sides of bacon in in a week besides all the little, which would be before your day, little picnic hams, they used to call them. And they used to be usually about eight pence to ten pence a pound. And everybody bought one for Regatta days and any special days that were going. Everybody brought a picnic ham. And we used to have about a couple hundred in just for these special occasion, or Christmas time. And we had a marvellous, marvellous trade over there. Everybody used to come to the Star.

But, of course, there was still Varcoe's, that is now. I mean, that was an old established firm. But for the cheap things they all used to come to the Star. Beautiful things they used to sell.

We used to do the window once a fortnight, dress the window. It'd be taken out Saturday night and then Monday morning, first thing, clean the window inside and out, and we had to dress it. And we used to have diagrams set of what you had to put in the window, you see, how to dress your window even in those days. And that would be done, and perhaps a couple come in to help the manager do that.

And then Monday afternoons you had to start on your baggin' up your stuff out the back. Two of you were sent out back to do the flour. The flour would come in two hundred-weight bags. Then there would be the two hundred-weight bags of sugar and the hundred-weight cases of cube sugar, lump sugar, that would all have to be weighed as well.

Currants would come in, and they had to be cleaned. Well, the errand boy usually used to do that. And they would be graded; the cheap ones, perhaps at sixpence a pound, would only be just broken up and rubbed through the sieve once. And then the next price would be an extra do. And then the better quality, the best ones, would have to be done thoroughly; so that they were really worth while. But they were all out of the same case.

Tea all came in in bulk; and you had to wrap that, weigh it and wrap it. And that had to be done properly, half pounds and quarters. And the baking powder, that all had to be done in screws. You had to do them in screws, that was quarter pounds and half pounds, and put in the drawer to serve the customers. Pepper, pepper was all done in ounces. And that all came in in bulk, and that would all be weighed separately. And the saffron in grams - you had to do that in grams, saffron. And everything you had that you can think of had to be weighed and wrapped - rice, sugar, all the cereals. And you see you had to wrap it right; so that there wouldn't be some runnin' out the pack. And best quality lard came in bags made of pigs innards, not plastic like today. You had all that to weigh up Monday afternoons.

And I always remember one Christmas. You see, fruit has the tendency of going dampish if the weather's damp. And we used to have an inspector would come down from London on certain occasions, and he would come unexpectedly on the doorstep at eight o'clock in the mornin' to make sure that we were there. He would travel down overnight from London to do his Cornish rounds of the shops. And one particular Christmas we had done up all this, you see, in pounds; so that you could get it quickly, you see, when you had your Christmas orders comin' in. And the funny thing was, he put it on the scales and found that they were a little bit overweight So he said, "What's the meaning of this? It will all have to be reweighed, repacked."

So the manager said, "Well, with the damp atmosphere they got a bit overweight. And do you know what he did to make sure that we did them over again? He poked his umbrella through every one, made a hole through every packet So that he knew that we'd have to rewrap them. See? So it wasn't easy bein' in a shop in those days. What we called him was nobody's business.

Election time was fun, very exciting. Course, they didn't come very often, as you know. I think it was every four years, same as what they do now, as far as I can remember. Well, we had lovely members put up for it. As I told you, we had Sir Charles Hanson for the Conservatives once. I think he got in twice, if I remember rightly. And he lived over in Fowey Hall, you see; so we were more interested in him, really.

And, of course, we had Isaac Foot, who was another very prominent man - well, he was a real orator, there was no mistakin' that. He was really it. He could put it over, and he got in several times here.

And everybody went, well, went mad for election time. The post-office used to be absolutely full. Boots hung up on the chimney. Mr. Simmons was proper politics. Mother used to pay a shilling a week all year around for shoe repair. Arch would take them up Saturday nights and didn't get home till eleven. They were talking politics.

And, of course, as the days grew nearer, they would hold meetings, you know. Wouldn't only be just the one meeting, but 'twould be on for several weeks before-hand that they would be all workin' up to that pitch. There was fighting. The men were as bad as the women. I remember in Fowey, there was an awful row down the street - girls fighting - Conservatives against Liberals outside the Church. I heard

Mrs. Barrett throwing dirty water on Mrs. Allen over the wall. In Polperro they dragged them up and down the river. They were more hot headed than Polruan.

And the Conservative one was always held out in the Battery Hall, that was the training place out at Battery Park, which, of course, is demolished now where that bungalow is built out there. Well, that was Battery Park, where the Naval Reserve men used to come and train once a year. I think they used to come from all over the area and train out there. And it was used for several things, but the Conservatives, they always held theirs out there.

And the Liberal one was held out West Street in the Wesleyan Sunday School that is now converted to flats opposite Mrs. Langmaid's. And it would be packed to the door. You never heard such a racket. Everybody would go to these meetings. And there was a gallery which I wonder never fell down with the stampede of the people stampin' their feet and all that. And there was also a platform where they would be on, which is all done away with now. And the platform would be full of people belongin' to the Committee, you know. All the old people of Polruan that were Liberals. Mr. Woodcock, you remember Mr. Woodcock, that died a little while ago. And then there was Mr. Allchin, a small man but a big Liberal man, always had a large yellow and blue rosette. He was the agent or somethin' for the Liberals in those days from out at Tredudwell. He was out at Tredudwell in those days. And then there was another man that lived up at Hall Farm called Roseveare; they were always big Liberals. And several people, besides, you know, that took part.

And I know one particular time we had a party came down from Plymouth, and they entertained us while we were waitin' for the member to come. Oh, songs and hornpipes; ladies and a gent came. Course, everybody was thrilled to bits with that. And eventually, cuz they were always late, you know, just the same as what they are now. You think they s'posed to come at 7:30; and sometimes it would be 8:30, perhaps, before they would arrive, stoppin' every place longer than they should stop.

Well, when we knew that they had arrived, well, you would have thought the roof was going to come off with the cheerin' and all. And they always used to be singin', "We know where our Isaac is,
He's at the top of the pile."

Well, when he came, it was - I don't know - it was like as if 'twas out of this world, you know, he sort of lifted everybody up to ecstasy, really. You thought that he was really somebody, which he was, really. He was a great orator, marvellous! And, of course, the other one was just the same - he had all his followers up there. Everybody used to go from one to the other. Opposition, nearly fighting but not quite, but just as bad. But it was more fun, really, you know. There wasn't that, well there might be a little bit of - what can I say - nastiness just for a day or two. But after it was all over. Well. That was the end of it, you see.

And we used to watch from home to see which flag went up, over Quiller Couch's where he lived, you see, or else at Hall, you see. Whichever one went up they would put the colours of the flag up to see who got in. So in the afternoon when the results came through, you see, everybody would be watchin' to see which party got in. Cuz there was no telephones an' that like there is today, you see. 'Twas all different . But it was really fun - we really enjoyed it, you know. Then afterwards, you know, after a day or two, we'd be all on friendly terms again, and everybody forgot all about it. But it was good while it lasted; it was really wonderful.

MAY JACKSON LANGMAID
BORN IN 1898, SPEAKING IN 1982, 1987

The Pills and the Climos had salmon seines here. My father, William Jackson, and others had a pilchard seine down Porthcurno before he moved here. He had to pull the boats up every night. Father strained his heart; so he moved up here with his cousins, the Dunns. Here the boats didn't have to be pulled up; they were kept on moorings.

In the picture of Fore Street Chapel, Granfer Dunn is in the doorway. The Dunn family came in the Year of the Blizzard, 1891. Shortly after he came, Father sat in Mr. Widlake's seat at Chapel by mistake. That was some welcome! So we went up Fore Street Chapel, which had a warmer feeling. When they were going to combine chapels and close one, Butcher Holton said at the meeting, "Think about it before you shut one. In Polperro they shut one, and some never went at all again." And when they did close Fore Street Chapel, that turned out to be true.

Father was a fisherman. He kept his nets and crabpots in an old store. He had trammels and crabpots; so we salted fish for the winter. In the summer, he took out visitors from Fowey Hotel. Only the gentry took holidays then.

I went out fishing with father in the daytime. We sailed or rowed out, and I helped pull the trammel nets in. But I didn't go at night when he went out Ludder Buoy pollocking. I also helped him bark nets in Dunn's yard. They used an old boiler which would bring brick colour. They made their own nets and made their own crabpots. For these they would cut withies at Mixtow and Trethake. Father was a cousin to Moses Dunn and Ernie Dunn. They all worked together.

We also salted butter, which was much cheaper to buy in the summer. We had butter from Mrs. Rollings from Pelynt. Mother salted it and kept it for the winter, then soaked it to get the salt out.

We lived at Burleigh House for twenty-six years. We had a lovely garden and orchard. We had chickens and two banties - we had no heart to kill them. But fishing was always unpredictable. We had to save for any poor weeks ahead.

Burleigh House was one house but had two doors always. On the left was the kitchen and stairs and back kitchen. On the right was the sitting-room, the whole width of the house, with a window both sides. Paraffin oil lamps were used in the home and in streets. There was one double burner lamp on the table by which we sewed and read. I still have the lamp. How we all saw to sew is beyond me, but we did. We had to make our own underwear, and I learned to crochet to trim my chemiscs etc.

We used the sitting room quite a lot. It had an open grate and polished table. Trammels and nets were made in the front room. Mother had a white table in the kitchen.

My sister and I slept together in the little bedroom. There was a tin trunk for bedding, and on top a cotton quilt cover. In those days, when I was a child, I wore a vest, calico chemise, gathered and smocked, calico knickers and a flannelette or woollen petticoat, white skirt with embroidery, then a dress and white starched pinafore over. We wore button up boots. Each of us had our own peg for our clothes.

Mother was from West. She used to wash down steps with a cloth. "'Tis Innocents Day, Wash all your friends away!" But she wouldn't wash blankets in May.

Manilla mats were done on sail canvas. First the rope was unturned. Then a stair rod or wood like it, a sail needle and palm were used. The canvas, about the width of a stair, was folded over and over and stitched over the rod. Some patterns could be made with darker and lighter shades, like a diamond shape in the centre. These mats were very hard wearing. You could scrub them. They were used instead of a rug on bluestone or flagstone or wooden floors.

Mother picked elderflowers, which she dried and steeped for elderflower tea for colds and inflammations. She also picked and dried angelica leaves. These were steeped for inflammations and were excellent. She poured boiling water over them and made a drink. You don't see angelica leaves any more. She had a herb garden. If someone was really sick, Dr. Boger came from Fowey.

One thing Mother used to make was 'heva' cake with figs. It was flat and rolled out on a sandwich tin with lard and big figs like raisins, which she stoned. She would roll it out and criss cross it like squares. That was 'heva' cake. Mother made it any time of year.

Mother made barm from boiling down hops and potatoes. I've forgotten exactly how she made it. She had to add a little of the old barm. If she had none left, she would send me for a ha'penny of barm from Mrs. Jacobs, who lived on West Street where Mr. Colliver lives now, two cottages past Tinker's Hill corner. The barm had to stand. Mother used a stone jug with a cork - the same jug Father used to take water in when he went to sea fishing. Sometimes the barm would make the cork pop. What a smell I remember, like yeast! Mother would sell the barm for rising cakes. People came with a jug to the door to buy it.

We children didn't do damage to things then. We all had our own jobs. I used to clean the knives on a special board, about seven by fourteen inches in size. I'd have a block of brick and rubbed the knives back and forth on the brick. This was done on Saturdays. The brick was like vim. If there wasn't a brick, you could get knife powder if you had a knife machine. You cleaned four at once. There were also shoes to clean.

At school we had Miss Plowie, then Miss Rundle after Mildred Roberts who became Mrs. Barnicutt. (teachers between 1902 and 1911). There was one big long room with no division and an ante-room at the back. The lighting was by brass lamps on a ratchet affair. One went up and one went down on chains. We had tip up desks with inkwells. Heating was by a big round bogie out from the wall and open fires. Toilets were slushed down every week with buckets. Newspapers were cut up and squared up for toilet paper. The Rogers from Triggabrown brought lunches; they were the only ones.

We brought our own material for sewing class. Copywriting was done by copying from books. The school didn't have a museum, but there was a library. Teachers didn't used to read aloud to us. When the Attendance Officer, Mr. Saunders, came we were given a silent reading lesson then. We always said Miss Roberts fancied him.

I didn't go to cooking class in Fowey. Mother always said, "Father and Mother can tell you all the cooking you want to know". You see, it cost to go cooking. You had to have an apron and cap.

Parents came to school concerts, which were dialogues and little plays. Once I was a nurse and made up a poultice for John Henry Salt. It broke, and John Henry had it all down his shirt.

We never had folk dancing in school. We had Drill. Knees outward and downward bend, hands on hips. Musical Drill was performed in circles and squares. Miss Roberts played the piano for that and there were songs with that.

44

We children played different games in different seasons. In winter we played with hoops and skipping ropes. The boys had iron hoops. In summer we played marbles in the streets and hopscotch in the field where Ceildhe and the Billings are, above Hockens Lane. We used to play in Hockens Lane. We built "houses" with stones laying out the rooms. But we weren't allowed to play on the Quay.

We also played ludo, snakes and ladders and draughts, but no cards. My boyfriend bought us a pack of cards once and had a talk with my father, saying that cards were no worse than ludo unless you gambled. We learned rummy then and played often. We also played rings. It hung over the door, and you threw rings over different hooks with numbers. I used to catch the rings that fell.

Mrs. Mitchell's shop was where Bessie Bate lived out East Street by the steps to Hall Walk, the front house. She had a partition across the front room, and the front part was the shop. She lived behind. She sold most things; paraffin, flour, moist sugar and bladder lard. This was lard in a pig's bladder and was considered better lard. We used it for the saffron cake we baked each week.

At Bartlett's shop next up from Corner Shop in Fore Street, old man Taylor had a paper shop before John Salt had his newsagent shop at Shipshape. After Taylor, Drew was a barber there. After him, the Drew girls had a draper shop.

I remember old Mrs. Pearn's shop on the corner. You would go in, and she'd say, "Sit down, my dear, and wait for the trader. He's out Punchy!" which meant that the 'Rival' hadn't arrived from Plymouth yet but was still at sea. Sometimes it was quite a wait. She'd have to come in and moor and unload before we could collect the goods.

On the first of May we would put garlands around our heads with a bit of curtain and make a cross. But girls pulled tin kettles around the village too, as well as boys. The council stopped it when the road was tarmaced. You see, baths and all sorts were towed around with one big rope. The boys were against it stopping. In fact, some of the bigger chaps picked up the policeman and put him on top of a water tank they were pulling around.

Harry and Carrie used to come to Polruan begging. Mother used to give them a copper. He had a concertina, and they used to sing "In the Sweet Bye and Bye". Harry had a pair of spectacles tied with a bit of string and an old trilby hat. They would go around through the streets. At Burleigh house there is still no inside sanitation, only a toilet by the gate (in 1982). We used to go in there to listen to Harry and Carrie.

Sometimes people from Pelynt would come and give concerts in Chapel. Afterwards they had concerts for the Liberal Party.

When I was in the choir, we used to have outings on a farm wagon with boards and go to Looe with two horses. Another time we went to Newquay in a wagonette with three horses with Mr Shopland, who used to drive for Fowey Hotel from Par Station. That was quite an outing. We had to change horses. Going across Gossmoor one of the horses took fright. It was very exciting! Mr Arnold James and

Arthur Bunt quietened the horses.

We often walked to Polperro. On Good Fridays they had Band of Hope at Pelynt, and we girls walked there.

In the Chapel Sunday School Hall, up Chapel Lane, there were two classes of the older children up in the gallery, which was bigger than now, about five or six rows across. One class was either side of the stairs. The stairs to the gallery used to go up the other side of the hall from the windows, against the wall. There were more classes, the younger ones, downstairs. There were no pews downstairs, only forms. At the far end was a platform, up three steps each side of the room with a desk on top. You could see where a rail had gone around.

Christmas time there was Darkey Partying. We would put on masks and dressing-up clothes and going carolling. Father used to dress Lil Stone up in an old jersey and trousers and me in a skirt of Mother's with the fullness in the back of the skirt pinned up with safety pins. We used to go only to the people we knew. Mrs. Wyett, in Moss Terrace, didn't recognise us and offered us ginger wine and cake. By the time we finished there was no chin to the paper mache mask we had bought for a penny or tuppence.

We always had a Christmas tree, a holly one with apples, and bought ornaments. I always had a white pinafore from Gran Jackson. I always hung my own stocking. I'd pretend I was asleep, and I would hear them say, " I don't believe she's asleep."

"Yes, she is. She's breathing steady." Then they'd fill the stocking. In it I'd have a few nuts, an apple, an orange, a little bag of sweets, perhaps a little packet of little starry biscuits and a toy on top, perhaps a dolly.

PERCY AND ANNIE CRAPP LIBBY
BORN IN 1901 AND 1900, SPEAKING IN 1978 AND 1983

(Mrs. Libby) My parents was born here, yes, all born here. Well, my father, Thomas Crapp was a sailor, used to sail in ocean going ships; he used to go to sea in 'Kohinoor'. Then he come home and went up the jetties as a docker. He done so much at sea when he was young, and then he come home.

Then he was in the Naval Reserve. Navy people were out Battery, you know, out where that bungalow is to. There used to be a big army hut. One part was for firin' guns at targets out where the Cannis Rock was to. That big wall what they put up - d'you know that big wall what was there? They took it down. Out where the look-out house is, down bottom Peak. Great high wall, it was, three times as high as it is now.

Well, there used to be a monument in the middle of the hill just above the new car park that they made in front of the NSA house 'n that (near St Saviour's Ruins). It used to be nearly so big as this kitchen. It had four or five steps to go up. I think Naval Reserve used to come here and lay on that one and put their target down to Fowey. There used to be big targets there, and they used to put the bull's eye on these big iron targets. And they'd be up on top of this here monument firin' at these targets, you see.

'N they used to come here. They used to pick up all the Naval Reserve from Looe, Polperro, Portwinkle, right down through. And they would walk; they would march here from all they places. They wouldn't ride. They'd be marchin', about seventy or eighty of 'em. And they'd come here for six weeks trainin'. And they had this here big hall built there. And they had a big iron what's-it-call in front of it with a hole cut in it fer the guns to go out through. And they used to fire at that target way out to sea in they days. 'N a lot of they women here married 'em. Yes, that's what they used to do.

(Mr. Libby) Father was from Talland, a farm labourer. Mother was from Polperro. In Polruan, my father became a dairy farmer. He was the only one, pretty well, there, supplyin' most of Polruan. He had this big dairy farm, that was eighteen dairy cows. An' he had about fifty acres of land way up top up where Mr. Bunt is to. He also had pigs, heifers, two hundred sheep and some chickens. I remember we drove twelve heifers and bullocks to Trago Mills. Two men and three boys met us who took them on the moors for the winter. There was more grass there.

Harvest time Mother had a dish enough to serve ten or eleven men. All of them came in for supper. It was the same at Triggabrown. There were potatoes and big hunks of meat. There was cider for the men at harvest. Pa got a big barrel from a farm. And there were big pasties.

My mother had, how many did she have? It was a good family, eight of 'em, I expect. There was a boy next to me, younger than me by a couple years. He was seven when he died. Then there was a maid between me next brother an' a sister. She was called Vida. She died. Y' know, they used to be babies in they days. Some of 'em were born dead, an' some would be born and live for a while, then die, in they day, cuz there was a different atmosphere in they days than it is now. See, there was no nurses here. There was women here that used to go around and do these jobs - just ordinary people, midwifes, they call 'em. But they used to do it.

I can remember Mother havin' - Mrs. Couch come when, I think, Peter was born, or maybe 'twas Richard. They always used to have somebody but never used to have no doctors. Cuz you couldn't afford it.

Now, like with whoopin' cough. Well, the children died of measles, didn' 'em? Me sister died of whoopin' cough. Up where Tommy Turner lives now, the doctor used to live there. He had a white horse, an he used to keep the horse in they stables underneath there. An' he used to have this horse for riding round to do his job, in they days, out around the country 'n everywhere on his white horse.

Then, of course, Mr. Thomas lived there. He had lovely cream, he used to have, oh lovely. We used to go up there eight o'clock in the mornin' for scald milk then, all they days ago. He used to come down from the hills, where Mr. Thomas keep his cows, out in the hills, down Fore Street, up Chapel Lane, over here 'n up the back o' that house, used to drive 'em all up that way. Then he had a field or two up top.

He milked 'em up top. The barn is gone now, all took down. You know the old small reservoir above the garage there, on the other side of the road? Well, a bit further up there's a gate on your right, i'n' there? Where you go in a field where they built the big reservoir. Well, right opposite that gate is where his old barns was. An' 'ee used to have a great horse called Jessie, di'n'a? An' then, the mess they used to make comin' in! An' that's why this gate was put here to keep 'em from goin' in Moss Terrace. Yes, they used to go in there. They knew where to go, they been there so many times, the cows.

Mother used to make oilskins from two hundredweight flour sacks. The sacks used to have a red and blue circle on them. She boiled them to get rid of the red and blue circle. Then she cut them out to shape and sewed them. Then she took linseed oil and a tin of yellow or black that you could buy and painted them all over to keep the wet out.

I was born in that house bottom corner of Chapel Lane where Mr. Jones is, there. Then we shifted from there down in the Co-op. Well, we had a tiny dairy, there where the Co-op is (now Polruan Supermarket). 'Tis all altered now. We used to have a passage way in through there then. Then there was a big kitchen inside where we used to live. There was a big farmer's range there.

We never used to sell all the raw milk in they days. They used to sell a lot, mind. But mother used to scald some of the milk to make cream, see. We had these big white enamel pans. She put four of these pans on this big stove, three parts full, of raw milk. An' it *was* milk in they days, 'twas good milk. 'N she put it on there. An' was stopped fer two to three hours until 'twas all crusted up 'n ready to take off. Then she had a little cloam basin, yellow outside, white inside, a little pastry bowl. Nice size one, y' know, to take all this 'ere cream up.

Now all that milk would be sold next mornin' - scald milk. And the people that used be lined up in that street outside the butcher's shop, it is now, was nobody's business. Buy a pint of scald milk fer a ha'penny, see. That's how they got rid of it, see. Cream, you couldn't keep that. People used to send here from away. Used to do it up an' send away to people. Pounds er half pounds, yeah. Course, it was cheap then, only six-pence. Well they'd have half one year. They'd be sendin' every year, see, when they knew about it. The Spring every year, it was.

Yes, we always had visitors. A different sort of people, y' know, we used to get, di'n' um? It was people who used to come year after year. It wasn't anybody who came on holidays in they days. It was middle class people, most of 'em. An' really, Father knew a lot of 'em cuz he used to have horses an' traps on the road then, takin' people to Polperro, Looe an' all that. See, he used to go in for that, too, see.

He had three carriages, and we had six horses. That's before the motor cars come out. And he used to keep two horses, "propers", fer bringin' stuff around to all the buildin' here. An' we used to land it all on the quay. Everything was landed on the quay in they days, thousands and thousands of bricks at a time. And my father used to go out around to where the buildin' was ever goin' on to. That's what he kept these two big horse fer. Another four was kept for on the road with carriages. He had a black one and a white one that was his carriage an' pair fer weddings 'n different things.

But before my father's time, there was a man called Werry, Farmer Werry. He used to live in that house right opposite the Co-op. You see that house up there with blue mahogany windows (No. 11 Fore Street)? You know, opposite the butcher. He used to keep that for his dairy. It was a big room in there in the bottom. I don't know if they parted it off or no, but it used to be his dairy and vegetable shop.

He had the farm what the farmer got that's where Mr. Butts is to now. Course it's all gone now from what it was then. An' the place other side of the road where Mr. Mitchell got, the pilot, that was a farm place. And that belonged to Mr. Werry. An' the place the other side of the road where Mr. Butts is was all houses there then, farm houses. It was early 1900s, might have been before, I don't know.

Father was here fer a couple year, attendin' masons as labourer. They built the Church up there 'n they place. And I suppose he was watchin' the masons workin'. An' he was only a labourer. An' eventually after he went off on his own.

There was an old man up here, a sharp man called Carnall, a farmer. An' he, he had china boats over with this ECLP there in Fowey, up Station, right up right opposite the car park at Caffa Mill, all that brick work building. Well, he used to bring all this corn from the farmers. And that'd go, be took across from Mixtow quay in a barge, took over there, an' all ground up ready for cattle feed; an' then he'd take it back again.

And my father borrowed seventy pound off him for to start off on his own. And the first house he built was where Jack Heard lives by the school. An' Mr. Lloyd Dunn's granfer, Moses Dunn, had that built. Then he went jobbing around fer several year. An', well, it couldn't have been very many years cuz I can just remember another one building on the end of it. The first one was nearest the school. I was too young to remember it building. But I can remember the second one growin'. But then he built Wellside, where Willie Hill lives. Then he built the Constitutional Club. And he weren't no tradesman. He just picked it up. He was tendin' labourer, mason mixin' up the concrete 'n stuff like that. He was just watchin'' what they was doin'. Then he built a house for Annie Roberts up here in front where Mrs Wilson lives there, at Florizel. 'N he built that place out in her garden. Only the house was there, but they had a piece put on. He built that. Father was illiterate, but he did all the building - plumbing, roof, all. Yeah, he had a lot of work. He was the only one here in they days. He was doin' a lot of work in Polruan. Everybody was after 'im. And he was a hell of a worker, and you had to do the same, see.

And I had a brother in they days, a lot older than me. He left school, course, an' went to work for Father. And he learnt the masoning too. Ernest Libby he was called. He was killed in the First World War. He was twenty-three when he was killed, and I was only about sixteen. Then I had another brother next to him. He

50

packed up 'n went out to Canada in 1912 or 11. Course, couldn't get on with Father, just left 'un.

And I had an older brother, called Sam. He runned away from the old man. They didn't know where he was to. But he was workin', too, couldn't get on. The old man was, really, he was hell. Hadda work so hard, he did. And, anyway, Sam was gone. They didn't know where he was to. It went on for weeks, 'n nobody di'n't hear a clue.

So there was an old man called 'Daddy' Smith. He was a sailmaker, lived up next door to Mrs. Broad, where she used to live, up past the W.I. in Fore Street. Well, he must have had people up in Exeter er somewhere around that area. And he was up there one time, an' goin' around, I s'pose, up there. So eventually, they had a letter from him, from this Mr. Smith. He was tellin' Mother, he said, "If you haven't found your son yet," he said, "I've already found him for you. He's up here with hobby horse people."

They couldn't get along. I expect he had a row with the old man. He was a youngster, afraid to come home, I suppose, cuz the old man, he was a heller, he was. Anyhow, that was that. Several weeks lapsed again. An' we still never heard nothin'. Course, they'd already contacted this hobby horse party. No, they didn't know where he'd gone. Next thing we heard, he joined the Navy as a boy, sixteen, fifteen. Well, things went on. He stopped away fer a bitty while. An' then, eventually, he did come home, ye know, 'n he stopped bein' in the Navy.

Father was an out and out Conservative. I left him, too, mind. I cleared out when I was sixteen. Yeah. And I had a brother. He went away in the Army. He joined up before he was of age, sixteen. Well, eventually, mother got him out of that cuz he was too young. When he was eighteen, he joined up again in the RAF. And after that, he comes out 'n went to work for somebody up in round Exeter, in the green grocery business. He was goin' around with a van sellin' this stuff.

Well, now, Father sends away fer 'ee to come home, then, to work fer un. But he was more - what's a call - than I was. I was a bit creasy, but he was more passive, if you understand. He kept on going, and, course, not long before father finished 'n turned it all over to him, the dairy. 'N he carried on. Willie, he was called Willie.

There used to be three boot repairers here; Mr. Simmons and Mr. Goldsworthy and Mr. Shepherd. Mr. Shepherd used to have a funny little shop - don't 'ee know the house out West Street, before you come in to the Chapel? That's what he used. Mr. Shepherd was livin' there, repairin' shoes there. Mr. Goldsworthy had where the cafe is down there now (No. 9, Fore Street). Below the chip shop, the first one below the chip shop. There used to be steps to go up, then to go in the front up from the street, not like it is now. They're all put away now, see. There used to be double doors there in the middle of that building. He used to sell shoes an' boots 'n all that, y' know. And Mr. Simmons sold everything; china, and boots, shoes - everything.

And we used to go out. We had a woman, here, called Miss Abbot. We used to go up there, have twopenny worth of pears. Lovely, when we was goin' to school, you know. She lived up in Pear Tree Cottage. They used to be hangin' over the wall. We used to knock 'em off with a stick. Her old man used to live there with a beard, 'n all that. Mrs. Abbot never had a shop, no, never had a shop. We used to go in her house. You know Mrs. Thomas lives up Fore Street (No. 20)? Well, the next house to that, this side. Well, you go in a passage. There used to be a baker's shop or somethin' years ago in back of that.

Men would catch all these fish and come in. And Mrs. Chapman, she'd clean 'em and marinate 'em. An' then we used to go down for six pennyworth of marinated fish. Like pilchards 'n that. That was years ago. You could always get a fish.

And then we had a little draper shop next door down there, Mrs. Roberts used to have, down there next door to Mrs. Chapman. That's down where Mrs. Hender got, see (Quayside). There used to be shops there, then.

Well then, up over Garrett Steps, going up from the Lugger, there was another little draper's shop. She was called Mrs. Blowey, an' she used to sell all sorts there. First house goin' up Garrett Steps. There used to be a big window there. This was Mrs. Blowey. She was a dressmaker. That house up there now, at the top of the steps. Jimmy Hicks used to live there years ago.

Mrs. Rollings, Sarah Rollings, would come to Polruan. She was come from Pelynt. She had butter 'n eggs 'n fowls, oh, turnips 'n apples, all that. She used to go with a little basket to some people, I s'pose. Father, uncle, I dunno, used to come with her. He used to come.

Then we had a man called Dickie Rowe sellin' fish. "New potatas, 'tata, 'tata new patatas," he used to shout. Then he used to come with strawberries from Polperro, always come down from Polperro. He was the brother of my mother, Dickie Rowe was. He used to sell on the corner or go around, yeah. Used to have a lovely little donkey trap. I donno how long he used to take to come. But he got here, anyhow.

There used to be a man come down from Lerryn here with apples. And we used to go an' take apples, 'n all sorts, that were in his cart, you know, an' run away. My, what fun we used to have! Got nothin' like it today, is there? Not fun like that. Back in they days, that was before 1914, all sorts we used to do there.

In summer we'd go down Newquay on the rocks to play. We'd catch clamieys with a pin on a string an' make boats with a bit of wood and ivy leaf an' dig limpets to catch fish on a bit of cotton.

First of May we used to go down in the cliffs under Lady Ram's - that's where they used to dump all the ashes in they days - and bring up all the tin kettles 'n buckets 'n all you could find. That's before the first of May, really, to get it ready for the first of May, an' bunch 'em all up together an' then pull them around the streets. That's before the streets were tarmaced, mind. They used to put stones in. You had to work 'em in with the cart and horse goin' up an down an' people walkin'. Big stones were half so big as your fist 'n cut your boots to pieces.

And, of course, we'd be takin' these tin kettles around only that day, wasn't allowed no other day. And the dust and stuff that 'ee'd leave behind. What the houses was like in they days, God knows. And there was an old bloke up there where the post office is now. That's Nigel Charman's granfer and brother, used to repair shoes in half of that place. An' they used to come out, you know, when we was comin' down, to try 'n stop us. Course, there'd be about two dozen boys down the end of this rope pullin' these things along. But 'ee could never stop it. See, when you got down, you couldn't see nothin' behind 'ee. It was all mud in they days. We had a big heap cuz there was plenty of boys. We'd come down the street, go walk out your way, West Street, get up around to the car park where the old school used to be, 'n turn around and back again down over the hill.

I remember Ringing Competitions. They were packed with people from all around. The Polruan set included my two brothers and Willie Hicks, Mr. Langmaid out Pont and Willie Tibbett.

Guy Fawkes there were big fires. Lots of furze in the hills was loaded on a barge from Carne. Father and I loaded it on the cart and pulled it up the hill. Four poles were put up to keep it from blowing away. Tar barrels, given by Mr Slade, were put in the middle on the bottom of the bonfire, sometimes where the playground is, another time in front of Watchhouse. They also had a bonfire down in Dunns' yard, yeah. Used to have a big one down there then. Oh my, everybody used to go down there. Fireworks were bought from Fowey. A squib was a penny. We would set them off around the fire. And you could get penny boxes of coloured matches, you know. You'd go around - they'd be pink or green or blue, you know. We never had the money you see.

Christmas, you wouldn't know it. You can't compare it now. We used to be out in they day, faces on, dressed up in old clothes, goin' around singin'. And all the old people be out, too, as could. Yeah, they'd be dressed up. Mrs. Lewis, down here where Len Brickell's livin' now, (No. 4) in East Street. She was a big woman. She used to come out with we. She used to be dressed up. She was a card, she was. Then there was a cousin down there called Mrs. Taylor. She used to be with a concertina, playin' lovely, where Mrs. Andrew is livin' now (No.10) in East Street. Course, everybody was in the same mind in Polruan then, cuz they's all Polruan people.

Then the men used to go around town and then go in the country, they used to. In the mornin' they'd come around collectin', you know, for some charity. They used to come out here about seven o'clock and go out into country, round all the farms, singin' carols. Then they'd come back about one o'clock an' go round the town Christmas Eve.

Oh, they was singin' all the time down there, You could go down there when 'ee liked, back in they days. You'd always see a couple of men down quay or up corner, there, singing every weekend. Course it went on and on, an' eventually the policeman would step in an' stop it.

Yeah, they used to be great Christmases in they day. They made lovely cakes for Christmas, saffron cakes, always used to have about eight er ten cakes in a tin. They'd bake 'em down Mrs. Parsons, you know. We always had saffron cake for Christmas.

Then we used to hang our Christmas tree up. Never put un up before Christmas Eve. But they get 'em up weeks before now, ain' um? We always had holly with the berries. We used to hang up gold an' all sorts, di'n' um, an' oranges. Used to hang up apples you know, on the tree. When the children come down Christmas mornin', they was delighted, you know, to see. That used to be more joy then and didn't cost nothin'.

We always used to have goose. They never used to get things like they do today. Well, to tell you the truth, we used to save coupons. There used to be coupons on Bournville cocoa, you know, then, years ago, and on tea. And on soap you'd get coupons, you see. Then we used to settle it up on boxes of chocolates fer the children.

And Boxin' Day, that was the day the men used to get drunk, then. Years ago, there wasn't many as didn't get over the bounds on that day. That was their day, Boxin' Day. People never had paid holidays then, no Christmas, no Whitsun, no holidays whatever. No holiday pay.

You know where that shop used to be down the corner of Quay Hill? There's a big window, isn't there? That was a school before all this was built. My father 'n all used to go there. You know Jack 'Wellie', Larrel Welsh's father? He told me he put his schoolin' time in there. They never had to go, really. But they used to go. I don' know if they had to pay or no. Tuppence a week, wa'n it? But that was the school, anyway, underneath that house. That was before any school was built. But this school up here, it's no more 'n a hundred years old, where the car park is to.

You don't take it all in when you're younger, do ee? Cuz your workin' with these men. You was apprentice, 'n they was older men, perhaps up forty, some of 'em there. You was workin' with un in the shipyard. You never took it all in, see. Oh, I've heard 'em say lots sometimes, different things. We was foolish really. Cuz they'd be a hundred now.

When I went to school, Mr. Widlake was very strict. He taught till he was well over seventy and also took night classes for boys who wanted to get on. Mr. Hobbs replaced Mr. Widlake when he was ill. He was a big man, strong and hard. At nine-thirty I went to school after the chores and cows. Break was at ten. The playground, then, was mostly gardens, only flowers. Six at a time would go out and tend them, those who were most interested. If you were interested in woodwork, you could go to Fowey for classes. There was a half hour for lunch. Perhaps we'd play football then or after four. One-thirty till four, it was drill in the playground, mostly exercises, not marching.

Electricity didn't come till the 1920's. In the school the roof beams were varnished. Lights hung from a cross beam and could be lowered down with a rope. There were three beams and three lights. The teacher's desk was against the wall. There was a Bogie stove, four or five feet high in the middle of the room for heat.

There was a little lean-to classroom for the seven year olds when they came up from the Infants' school. Miss Slade taught them. I remember, when a boy was caned, dust would fly out his coat at the back. Desks were ten or eleven feet long, four in a row, with the seat fastened to the desk and ink pots in the top. We all would queue up outside before we went in. We called out by numbers and toed the line. Toilets were outside against the wall in from gate of car park.

Mr. Roberts took the boys out to play football. He was very likeable, and mixed well. Mr. Tippin' was well educated and more on Parish council and Liskeard District Council. He was a gentleman.

There was a Sunday school up near the Club (Old Schoolhouse now) when I was a youngster. We used to go there to Sunday School. Then, come eleven o'clock over to the church. Well, Sunday in they days was like goin' to a school daytime. Your parents made you go. 'Twas natural that you went every Sunday. Never had to ask nothin' about it cuz you knew you hadda go. An' it'd be full up with children, fifty or sixty there in the Sunday School. There was an old lady used to come across from Fowey teachin'. An' Mrs. Annie Roberts, up Florizel in they days - her father was captain of a ship - she used to go up there teachin' children. An' there was somebody else in Polruan used to go up there. Mrs. Brown, she was a sister to Willie Hill's father. She used to live up that house up top of School Lane there, Hill House. She used to be a teacher up there.

Old John Salt was the caretaker at the church. The one who kept the shop down bottom there where the telephone kiosk is to. That used to be his shop; an he used to sell papers, sweets, and tobacca. He'd go out around the town, Town Cryer, ringin' the bell eight o'clock every day. That's the bell you see in the Readin' Room wall.

This place, in they days, if I tell you the truth, was full of captains of vessels and sailors and dockers and shipwrights. That's all this place was full of in they days. Well, there were several vessels owned in this port. Most captains lived this side. There was Cap'n Stone and Cap'n Martin. Cap'n Stone lived up Tinker's Hill, in the gate, not up over the step. Then he shifted up Fairview in Tinker's Hill. There's a bungalow built on the end of it there, where Mrs Butts used to live. You know, Mrs. Stone died there. Providence Place. They lived there, the Stones.

I remember Cap'n Stone an' his wife goin' up in a little pony and jingle, goin' up through Fore Street. My, only a jingle! He was the coal merchant, an' he used to take his wife out in the afternoons, and he'd go up street with this little jingle. Mr. Tommy Stone.

Cap'n Martin lived up top of Tinkers Hill, where the girl Tomlin lives now, Betty Tomlin. Up in the row, opposite the Club there. That big row of houses there. He owned his ship called 'Ada Peard'. Nice big ship, four hundred ton. Then there was captains up here lived in they houses where Fred Charman's house is, two of 'em there livin'. Then there was Cap'n Tadd, lived up where Lynches livin', in Moville, up top of the hill there. Then we had a Cap'n Brown who lived up here in the first house.

Then he had sons come along, they was captains. They all had sons took up the sea in they days.

We had one Slade here. Cap'n Slade. He had the 'Ada Peard'. He lived out there bottom Tinkers Hill where the guesthouse is (Waterfront Apartments, divided into two houses, then). He lived in the first one comin' up from the steps. And Cap'n Roberts he lived in next one nearest this way. Then we had a Cap'n Roberts lived up here where the Bates live on Moss Terrace, another brother. Then we had a Cap'n Roberts up here in Florizel; he was another brother. All cap'ns of big ships.

Then we had Cap'n Cundy lived in the first house here, Moss Terrace. He was another cap'n of a big ship. He was took prisoner in the First World War. Then we had Cap'n Smith next to Mr. Bedale (Penhaven in East Street), he was another captain, Stanley's granfer. Then we had Cap'n Slade, used to keep the Russell Inn. He had the coal store down quay by the Lugger, outside the Lugger, where the garages are? Cap'n John Bate, he was a nice man. He had it fer years. It was his own property, I think, cuz his father had it before him. John Bate Slade, he was connected with the Robertses; they was all intermarried an' all. Cuz he married - I think he married a sister of Cap'n Roberts. And then another sister of John Bate married Cap'n Jim Roberts up here in Florizel. Oh, it was all Cap'ns here in they days. There was more 'n that if you think on un, you know.

I knew the lot of 'em. I used to go around this village with milk when I was a boy. Before I went to school, yes, in the mornin', I used to, half past five. Went to school half past nine. I used to carry around milk. I was six to seven year old, I was. I used to have three cans, used to measure it out in these cans. It was all measured into cans. Fer certain people, see. Back again, fill up again, out again. Yeah. Used to milk all the cows up there where Cap'n Hill built the house there at Sunnyside. Willie's son lives there, don' he now? Well, that used to be our old barn again for milkin' cows. Always milked the cows there. They finished with it when it burnt down. That finished it.

Now, there was a man called Mr. Clogg, farmer, where Hamilton Pearce got now up there, Townsend Farm. That was Mr. Clogg in my young days, and he used to kill his old bullocks up there on the farm. One of his houses is on the farm now. And his butcher's shop was next to the Russell. He had quite a few sons, this Mr. Clogg. Some went up the dockyard as shipwrights. Some was captains of ships. And others went out to Canada, one or two. He was a great big man, six-footer with a beard.

Election time used to be all hell here, in they days. And we had a man here called Danner Hicks, that was Willie's father. Sir Reginald Pole-Carew was the Tory and Sir Edgar Barts was the Liberal. Well, this Willie's father used to carry this 'ere Pole-Carew on his shoulder. He was a Tory. There were a lot of Tories here, then. Most people were, you know. My father was a great Tory. He was an awful Tory. You don't see that today. It used to be murder here.

We wore great rosettes, red, white, blue. Yes, always knew who was what. All the shops, they'd get annoyed. Oh my, I dunno. A Liberal wouldn't go into a Tory shop, or the other way around. Too much of it in they days. Michael Tomlin's grandad used to repair the boots. He was a great Liberal. And my old man and 'e, he had hell up with 'e. I can remember back when I was a boy down where 'e was workin', used to be hell to pay. Then you'd see posters up - the Tory, perhaps, with a big battleship and a big loaf posted up everywhere, anywhere around here. Then the other party would have somethin' else up, yu know, 'gainst it.

They used to go down Quay eight o'clock in the mornin' to meet un comin' across from Fowey. They had the Battery out Peak there (where Hoe Cottage is now). That's where all the electioneers used to speak out there, where all the political meetings was held. An I've seen em there havin' a scuffle out the door. It used to be awful.

On Election Day there was no wireless nor nothin'. Whoever got in, they used to look over Fowey an' see what flag was pulled up. If the Union Jack was up, the Tories got in. If the Liberals got in, just the same. Different flag, blue and yellow, I think it was. It was a different flag. But it used to be come three o'clock or four o'clock in the afternoon. They was all eyes over there then.

When I was sixteen, I went in the shipyard, an apprentice. That's when we caught the whale. We went up to where the car park is up to the station there, Caffa Mill. That was the shipyard. Mr. Heller, he was the shipyard owner then. He had a brother called Willie; there was two of 'em. I used to work for William Langman. I was pickin' up about five bob a week apprentice money, an' no money overtime.

Mr. Slade used to have where Jack Toms got his boat yard now. So one day he seen me there, an he stopped me. "Here," he said, "You want a job?"

I said, "Well, I dunno," I said. "I gotta see somebody else about that. I can't just leave it 'n run away."

He said, "I'll give ee a job." He said, "How much do you get an hour up where you're to?"

I said, "Five bob."

He said, "I'll give ee more 'n that." An', well, I told mother about it, an' she agreed. Cause that'd save me from goin' across the water. To go to work then, I hadda leave here seven o'clock. 'Twasn' like it is now, y' know, goin' work eight o'clock, nine o'clock. Seven o'clock I was goin' up the river no matter what the weather was. An' we put in forty-eight hours a week in they days; that's a week's work.

'N I stopped here, then, till everything went bust, went bankrupt. I just managed to finish me apprenticeship. You know Mr. Carter over Fowey, the broker that used to be. He owned a big ship 'ere called 'AB Charman'. We used to keep her up Pont. That's where we was doin' the repairs to her, big job. She was here about three year, and that finished the shipwrightin'. There were little bits of jobs after, but they couldn't do the big jobs; they never had the money.

An' while we was up Mr. Heller's was when we caught this whale, see. Well, we was only boys. We never see no danger in it. But there was danger in it, you see, cuz we was only young. We never thought nothin' 'bout that. We went after un, caught un off up Bodinnick, there where the ferry is. We come up there one dinner time, 'n laid out oars, 'n we had a big boat 'n stopped. An' 'twasn' very long before this whale come up right alongside the boat. 'Twas about thirty feet long.

Sammy Dunn, tha's a Polruan boy, he was up harbour there in the bow of the boat with a harpoon; an' she come up. She had never a chance then. He just stuck 'n in the tail, you know. Away she goes up the river, hauled us right up Golant, yeah. Yeah, right up there. Dockers was all there workin'. They stopped. They didn't know what was happenin'. They couldn't see nothin' towin' of us. They just seen the rope out, that's all. Then the train was comin' down. That one stopped, too. Stopped up Golant, up above Golant. We was there stopped about ten minutes. We didn't know what she was doin' or what was happenin'. She came down, went right across the river, Polruan side. There was a little beach there. She went in on this beach. You can tell how fast she was goin'. She was goin' so fast she heaved herself three parts out of the water.

Yeah, the boat come right in right in on top of it. Course, it bein' greasy and slippery, we slipped. Some went overboard, out over the stern. Course, I s'pose they weren't expecting somethin', y' see. Anyhow, that was that. So we started tryin' to kill un there.

We thought we'd killed un. But there was two Army officers there convalescin' over Golant, First World War. They come over dressed up in their sharp tunics, y' know. The sharper one of the two, he said, "You got to kill it now."

I said, "Yeah."

"Well," he said, "I'll show you how to kill it."

I said, "All right." There was a bit of a bar there. So he stuck this 'ere bar down the blowhole - they got blow holes in um see. When they come up, they blow for air. An' he stuck this one down. Before he had a chance to say 'Nellie', up she goes like a fountain, blood, mud, gore, all sorts of colours like a fountain. You never seen nothin' like it - blood, black, green, every other colour. He was just simply lathered with it.

We thought we killed un. We lashed her up to the bottom of the boat, when the tide come in again, an' started to come down. Well, we got over Saw Mills, up river. Well, right opposite that, an' the boat wan' no more than that freeboard with the weight of this one underneath her, see. An' we was pullin' four oars, pullin' up there. An' when we got down salt water, the boat started to move, see. She come to life again. Well, then we put all the four oars one side, caught hold of 'er, an' pulled as hard as we could. An' we got down opposite No. 8 Jetty and got in on the beach again there, Polruan side. So we did kill un there then.

That evenin' we brought un down Polruan quay. And where the people come from that night, God knows, I don't. Come from everywhere, must have. There was only one boat here at the time, carry twelve - ferryboat. But they come here somehow. I don' know where they come from. It was full up with people here, to see this thing.

There was a man here called Colfield, oldish man he was. He was the Naval officer in charge of the port in the First World War. He was a heller too, yu know. He came up around. "Anyhow," we thought, "we catch it now." Cuz we ain't s'posed to be on the water, see, in they day. I don' know what they could have done to us.

And he come down off the beach. He said, "What you boys doin' here?" Well, we thought we was in fer it now, see, cuz 'twas restrictions on the harbour, see. He said, "Get a sail an' cover it up an' make people pay to look at it." We never thought like that, see.

Well, we took it up on Carne Beach, up Pont there. Well, there was a man called Harvey used to live down where Whitewall Randolph does now (Newquay House). He had been in charge of the factory in they days. 'Twas the sardine place for fish that they used to bring here. Course it was a big place. They used to can it down there an' all. That was before my time, see. Anyhow, he said he'd like the tail. He would take it up Brazen Island and cure it, see. Course it was hell of a - it was seven foot six across.

So, well, we cut un off, pulled it around there, an' pulled it up on the quay fer un, an' put it away where he wanted. But what happened to it, I dunno. We never heard, really. Then we took the fish up Carne beach. And some of the fishermen here in they day, they cut it up fer cod bait. I believe they had most of it, really. That's the story of it all.

RUTH WYATT SETZ and
DAPHNE WYATT TAYLOR
BORN IN 1901 AND 1906, SPEAKING IN 1978

Mother was born in 1870 in Phyllis Turner's house, Albany House in Chapel Lane. We lived in Limestone Terrace before Rosemary House. Rosemary House had two rooms in the dairy part, made into a sitting room and toilet (unusual then) and four lovely bedrooms upstairs. Percy Libby's father had it as a dairy.

Now Ruth, our young days. First of all my mind goes back to when it was a penny return from Fowey on the ferry boat. And many a time we didn't pay the ferry when we rowed across ourselves. We took an oar, and the ferryman sat back and enjoyed his pipe. And when it was rough, there were four oars; and we'd be two girls and the one man, a girl on each oar and one man, as I remember.

And then, when four men formed a company and got a new motor boat and wanted to put it up to a penny each way, the natives wouldn't pay it. But it was well worth it because it was Captain Walters from Looe. He started the first motor ferry boat. And there was court case, and Isaac Foot was judging the case. And he had a strong following of Liberals in this area. So he decided to split the difference, and he made it three ha'pence return, remember?

And do you know we as shop girls would say to Captain Walters, "Take us for a trip." And he would take us around the ships in the harbour, or he would take us as far as Castle. Even if people were waiting on the quay, there was never a word said.

If you wanted to catch a train at Fowey station, you had to leave about an hour beforehand because the ferry would take so long. And for two shillings, a ferry boat would take you up to the station, up to the Ferry slip. And the ferry-man would carry your cases to the Passage slip, and he would carry your cases from door to station, for two shillings. Now-a-days they wouldn't do that to come to your door just to speak to you.

And when the people would jump out of the ferry, a little impatient, they'd get on the gunwale, jump out with their back foot that was on the gunwale, and push the boat. And the boat would go right out, and it would have to be manoeuvred back again. And then the next one that was come in would get on the gunwale, jump out, push their foot back again; and out would go the ferry again. Oh, it went on like that. It was cruel, really.

Talking about politics now, Isaac Foot was well known in Polruan; and, of course, Pole-Carew, he was the Conservative candidate. Pole-Carew one generation and Carew-Pole the next generation. Yes, that is so. And do you know, the parents almost used to fight over politics? And I doubt if they knew the first thing they were arguing over. We used to wear rosettes, every one of us, as big as a dinner plate.

I remember, when the Conservative Club was opened, my parents, staunch Conservatives always, going to the Conservative luncheon. And each of us laid a foundation stone and all dressed in our best. It was a great occasion in the village.

And do you remember the school days of long ago? Going to school with all our lovely, white, starched pinnies on. Oh, you always wore a pinafore.

When we saw a car coming at ten miles an hour, we'd run to see. I was about fourteen. It was very exciting. Sam Libby had the first one. It crawled along.

Jack Simmons, father of May Charman, had the first motor-boat. They used to go up Lerryn river, to Penpol especially, for picnics - lovely saffron buns. I was a young teenager.

And our father, Captain William Wyatt, was a sea captain at that time. He brought lots of presents home, didn't he? We used to love to wait and see the ship sailing in full sail till she got to the Castle. Then down it would all come. Then over the side would go the ship's boat, and the sailors would bring Father in with all the parcels. Oh, grand times!

My father brought the first gramophone to Polruan from Germany. The first record was "Laughing Policemen". A little crowd would gather outside the house to listen.

Of course, it was always a Red Letter Day when Father came home, and we were all taken to Fowey to Mr Pikes, the tailor, to be measured up for little tailored suits and to the bootmaker to be measured for high button boots. I remember that well. Mother's favourite colour was Parma violet. She always used to say to me, "There's no colour to me like Parma violet." And snowdrops were her favourite flowers.

And on one occasion, when she was going away to stay on a ship with my father, only up to Plymouth in Millbay Docks, she was going to stay just for two days. And I remember her walking down the street beside my father, who was a very big man with a black beard, typical sailor, more like a smuggler, you might say, all dark. In fact, a certain Mr. Clotchard said he was the most handsomest man he'd ever seen, he'd ever measured for a new suit. He always thought he was a very handsome man. That was by the way.

Mother loved Parma violet and had a beautiful suit made, and it went in at the waist like a wasp waist, and it was long, and the jacket was long, and the reveres were velvet. And she always wore a toque like Queen Mary. In fact, she would remind one of Queen Mary. I'll show you some photos one day. Well, she loved little toques just like Queen Mary. And she used to go on board, and she'd go away dressed like that as though she was going to a wedding. Nowadays they would go aboard ship in a pair of old jeans and not think about dressing up at all.

But they had to go into these brokers' offices, all these captains' wives you know. There was a lot of competition with big hats, and fancy dresses and rings all the way up to their knuckles, as Mother used to say. Mother always used to say they had rings right up to their knuckles.

We all had trips with father. My mother was rather dry at times. You could laugh, you could laugh at some of the sayings. And there was a second lady in the village, and every time she met him she made a point of shaking hands. "Oh hello, Captain Wyatt."

Every time Mother would sniff, and Mother would say, "Now get ready, get your hand ready." every time before she met this lady. She used to say, "Now get your hand ready." It was so funny, and Mother knew it was coming, and so did we - but these things come back to you.

And Mother would go to sea with four girls and a boy. And we were told to be seen and not heard. And there was never one bit of bad behaviour. We were to do as we were told, and we did because I'm afraid our mother was rather strict, although one of the very best. Well, they had to be, di'n't they? These days are so different now, aren't they?.

To occupy their leisure time on board, the seamen would make mats, first of fibre and sisal, later of wool. You remember the old stair rods. Well, they would use one of those, or perhaps it was a special rod for mats to keep the rows even. Later, when they used wool, they would get large quantities of it in different colours. I think they worked from the centre out to make a pattern, sewing with the wool on lengths of canvas. All seamen's houses had these floor mats. Those on the floor were washed by their wives and kept as clean as table-cloths.

Mother told us about one storm, either in her day or in her mother's day, that was so bad that all the windows in Polruan were blown out. And they hung up these mats, of Philippine straw, over the windows to keep out the weather!

Captain Martyn Tadd wrote in "Sea Breezes" about record passages made by the my father and the fruit schooner trade. He commanded 'Uzziah' several years and had shares in her. Once he sailed with a cargo of 350 ton of salt from Cuxhaven, Germany to Plymouth, 722 miles in 72 hours despite the fact he had to deviate to keep clear of German warships in battle practice. That was a speed much faster than majority of coasting steamers - I believe it was a record.

We would be given about sixpence to go over to Fowey for the Fair. And then, out of that sixpence, we would bring back Mother sugared almonds, pink and white, or some peppermint rock. That was Fowey Fairing. You never went to the Fair without bringing home some fairing.

And as children, we always had plenty of things to do. I never saw groups standin' up there, nothing to do, like they do now, saying they're bored cuz they have nothing to do. Cuz we had hoops and tops and spinning tops and marbles and diablo and they had hopscotch. And there was one time we had a craze for all the girls havin' a broom handle. And we would have a competition as to who could jump with the broom handle furthest. Do you remember? And we used to call ourselves Girl Scouts because, I think, Boy Scouts at one time had broom handles. I don't remember if they had broom handles or a proper stick. But we had broom handles as girls.

Do you remember when the Sea Scouts came and they were down at the old watch house down at the Castle? Of course, years ago there used to be Royal Naval Reserves in Polruan. And every time I'm out Peak now, sitting on the seats, I can remember when they had the firing range down on that very long wall they've got down there at the bottom of Peak, and the targets would be put up. And to this present day the boys are down digging out the bullets. I was only out there last week, and the boys were digging on the wall, and the boy Perkins showed me the bullet that he had dug out of the wall, which might have been fired by our own father back in the days when he was in the Naval Reserve.

And he was stationed at the old Battery out at Peak, which unfortunately was all dismantled and taken to Fowey and built as the present Armoury. I never knew anything so silly. Polruan people must have been foolish in those days to allow a beautiful Battery, like we had out at Peak, taken down stone by stone and taken to Fowey. Disgraceful!

They used to have lovely balls out there, dances. You don't remember that but I do. I'm a few years your senior, unfortunately. I try to think I'm still fifty-nine. But that's by the way.

We used to have threepenny hops, yes threepence on a Tuesday in the old Church Hall. Tuesdays and Thursdays threepence. And Saturdays for sixpence.

There used to be wonderful concerts in the old Church school hall - wonderful plays, beautiful dresses. And we used to have Magic Lanterns occasionally. A man would visit. He'd be at the back and we'd see pictures which moved - very jumpy but amusing. They were 3D - it was before cinema and funny, like comic strips.

Years ago, they tell me - I can't remember so much - but years ago they tell me there were between thirty and forty shops in Polruan. I can't think how it would be, but that's what I've been told. I doubt if many people now can remember the shop that was definitely in Tinkers Hill, just down from Top o' Tinkers. That was a lovely shop. And we always used to have good measure because the Abbots - the eldest daughter was engaged to my brother - and that's why we always had good measure. Yes, I always remember that. She was called Leonora.

Then poor old Grannie Chapman on the Quay. She used to sell ha'pence worth of licorice, poor old soul. She was so crippled in hands and feet with rheumatism. Oh, lumps on her hands when she'd be serving out this bit of licorice. Then the lovely drapery shop next door.

And then there was the beautiful chemist shop out West Street. That belonged to Charlie Stephens and his wife. I did some knitting for her.

Shipshape had the door the other side then. John Salt, a cripple with one arm and one leg twisted, sold lovely sweets there - not home made ones - especially Rowntree gums and Cadbury coconut. The bank had the window altered to how it is now.

Nicie Thomas lived in the bakery which was a private home then before Mr. Hunt. She sold bags of chips, pasties. She was called Nicie because she sold nice things. She made rock - she threw it around, had a bench with a hook and would pull it. She was a huge woman and old. She was grannie to Charlie Thomas.

Do you remember, years ago, poor souls, when they were being buried, they were carried from Polruan out to Lanteglos by teams of men, and they would take over, different ones, every telephone pole or somethin' like that. They had sets of men, six in a set, rain or fine, summer or winter out to Lanteglos from Polruan about a mile and a half. Yes, and when Papa was ill, just for a fortnight, there was all straw and hay in the street to deaden the sound. You never see that now, never.

Mrs. Parker, the Vicar's wife, was buried at sea in 1930 five miles south east of the harbour. The coffin was plain oak with a blue lid bade for by Mrs. Parker. Choir girls from Church followed the cortege to quayside, wearing blue veils over their dresses. She said no one including relatives should wear mourning and there should be no flowers. They all sang her favourite hymns. Hundreds of people were present. At two in the afternoon a waiting launch went out for committal of her body. As she sank covered with pall, five wreaths were dropped in the sea.

On Fridays, about lunch times, or dinner times as we called it then, there was a man came down from the country. He used to sell lovely apples by the gallon, and he had Winter Stuppers. You never see Winter Stuppers. They've gone out of

64

fashion now. Haven't seen Winter Stuppers for years. So we used to wait until he was delivering, about half a dozen of us girls, and we each wore a beret. And when his back was turned, we helped ourselves to some Stuppers and put them in our berets and then went on to school.

And on Friday evenings we were given a ha'penny, and what we could do with that ha'penny!

Course, we used to have wonderful days on the 1st of May, when we would go for a river trip at dawn right up Fowey river and then come back. And the boys would have tin kettles. Their parents would save them every kind of tin and kettles and drums and any sort of tack. And they'd drag them around Polruan streets, up and down and all around.

And they used to go wild on the quay. I remember on one occasion Dickie Helman's father, he was the policeman, and he was standing in front of me on the quay. I just gave the back of his helmet a tilt over to the front. My goodness, he chased me! He didn't catch me though.

And then the girls would have hoops that they would cover with greenery and put in any flowers and bits of ribbon and bits of coloured paper. And we'd go around singing songs just like they do carols now and collecting money. It used to be beautiful, beautiful.

I don't remember any May Carols but t'would be proper things suitable - just as carols are suitable for Christmas. There would be suitable songs and lyrics for the May Day. It would be lovely, all these garlands. And some would have like half hoops instead of a whole hoop. Some would have half hoops draped and hold it like this. Oh, I remember that so well! And we'd be singing at doors and getting money for it. Beautiful, all in white aprons; and if we had on our best ones, there would be ribbon threaded through the broderie anglaise all along the yoke and up the arms and across the back.

And then on every 1st of April, that was what was called April Fools' Day. It was funny. In the mornings you could April Fool people because you would tell 'em to look, and unsuspecting they would look, and of course there'd be nothing there. And then in the afternoon you could 'tail pipe' people with all sorts of 'tail pipe'. You'd get a long bit of string or a long bit of rope or a long bit of ribbon with a pin. And when people weren't lookin', you'd pin it on their backs. And they'd go around with this tail on, not knowin' it for the rest of the day. And nobody would tell them. It would be so funny to see them goin' around. And this one would be laughin' at that one with a tail, never knowin' that they had a tail themselves. It was one of the funniest things because nobody knew that the other one...and they all think they was laughin' at somebody else. And they all had a tail.

You belonged to the church, and their annual treat was a trip to Spit Beach. That was latterly. The Sunday School Treat before that was to the old Vicarage, where you could pick your own strawberries, and sugar and cream would be provided. That was when the Vicarage was in the country out at Pendower. But when that finished, our Sunday School treat would be to Spit beach. That's just outside Fowey just along the coast by Par. And that was a wonderful day to Spit Beach. Today they would want to go to London or somewhere, wouldn't they?

On All Souls Day, they would have a procession from St. Saviour's Church out to Castle through Peak. The vicar, choir in surplices, and everyone who wanted to would go. There would be prayers and a bunch of flowers was thrown on the water.

Rogation Day was in Spring always on Sunday. Open Air services were held at Lanteglos church. We'd go outside and say prayers for a good crop. Everybody would bring something - bits of iron, blacksmith's tools - all were placed in the cemetery just before the step in front. We would all sing Rogation hymns inside, have our service, then go outside.

It seems to me, looking back over the years, the one thing that sticks in my memory is that I never remember bad weather. It always seemed fine. We always had nice summers. And the funny thing was, the things we were given as children. Our parents would boil what they called crabs and scerriwigs, and that would be spider crabs. And each child had their own little hammer and their own little parcel of crab. And we'd all go out in the meadows and sit down. And we'd crack all our crabs and pick them out, eat them, put all the bits back, and bring them home in the same bit of paper. And then the parents would have had no smell in the house. We would enjoy, each of us, our own spider crabs. It would be lovely and our own little hammer and little skewer. And it would be a real feast to go on like that. Now our best meadows are all ploughed in and houses built on 'em.

Course, the one thing I regret is they lost the rubbin' stone up in Meadow Way. The developer, he was told to preserve that stone. And when we looked, we couldn't find it. But someone will find it in their garden one day. They just ploughed it in. That was a shame, you know. It was a great big rubbin' stone. Older people told stories about it being a memorial. But in latter years they said that the cows used to rub themselves on it. So, therefore, we knew it as a rubbin' stone. But the old people thought it was one of the Druids' things and had some sort of ceremony there. That's as it may be. As the years have gone down, someone has lost these connections.

We were never allowed out late at night though. No, because there were no lights in the streets. It was pitch black. No lighting at all!

All the courting couples took walks Sunday evenings, meeting their boy friends after Church or after Chapel. And as soon as they got a bit serious, they would each go to Church or Chapel together. You knew it was gettin' serious if they went to Chapel or Church on Sunday evenings together. After that you could expect to hear wedding bells. Being a seafaring place, sailors would come in and marry some of the girls; but I, for one - we were always Church people - I married a staunch Wesleyan from a Wesleyan family.

Gutters were always running with water, what with people throwing out waste, and streets so rough. You know the taps were in the streets for the water. Years ago they had to go to the wells for the water. How dreadful that must have been, especially the washin' for washin' lettuce or salads. There was a pump in the corner, there was a well in the top pub, there was a well out in Dunn's yard. There was a well down Newquay, I remember, still down there. Have you seen the well down Newquay (in Tom's Yard)? Lovely, all with arched things. And in Paul Bedale's back garden there is the arch now of a well that used to be there. When he's got time he's going to unearth it to see if it's still there. And there was a well at Wellside. That was where the cattle drank. So people at the top went for their water there.

And could you imagine Polruan, coming up, looking at seven or eight cows - `omaybe nine or ten. They were coming down Fore Street to go up Chapel Lane to go in the stables up there to Mr. Thomas, the dairy man, to be milked, yes, in the cow shed to be milked. And you'd come up Fore Street, see the cows coming down, oh dear. He would have a can of scald, scalded milk, and a can of real fresh milk. I can remember the cans hanging on the side of the can inside. There was a half pint measure and pint measure. And course, by the time he'd slopped the measure up and slopped it back into the jug and all the dribbles back, I don't think there was ever any fair measures.

And we would be sent for our saffron for Mother to make saffron cake, always on a Friday, a gram of saffron. I don't really know the price now; but I'd like to have it compared. I think it would beat the ferry prices for inflation. That was a Cornish expression, "as dear as saffron" at that time. It's always been one of the dearest things because, as you see, it weighed so light.

Good Fridays and Easter Mondays, all in a group with our sandwiches, we'd walk to Polperro and back. I think it's eight miles to Polperro. And the roads were awful, pits and puddles. Do you remember the last time we walked down there? I said to you, "This chap coming on his bicycle looks so much like a man from Scotland." We were taking a walk with our children to Polperro one afternoon and I said, "Doesn't he look like Bob Lithgow?" That was a friend of mine in Scotland. And he cycled right by, and he looked, and I looked. And then he stopped, and we stopped, and there it was. It was actually Bob Lithgow, cycled all the way from Scotland down. So he said, "We will come into Polruan and get accommodation for the night, and we can see you when you come back." So we carried on. Isn't that wonderful to take the children for a walk to Polperro and back because it was a nice day?

VIOLET EDDY TABB
BORN IN 1902, SPEAKING IN 1987

I was born in Golant eighty-five years ago, and moved to Lombard Mills when I was two-and-a-half. Our furniture was taken there by boat. Father was a house decorator. We had a small holding of twenty-five acres; and we kept cows, chickens, calves, ducks, geese, turkeys, everything.

We had five cows at Lombard Mills. You could do anything with them. We never chained them to milk them. One of these cows was black and was called Smutty. One day Smutty was lying down in the yard. I was just three years old at the time. I had a bucket and was 'milking' her. My father came in the yard and saw me sitting by her. He was afraid to say anything for fear Smutty would move on top of me. He came up quietly to me and pulled me away. "Never do that again," he said. "That cow could kill you!"

"She wouldn't hurt me."

"She wouldn't on purpose, but she could easily roll over onto you!"

We had a broody hen one time. Pa asked if I had got a clutch of eggs - that would be thirteen. I had twelve, but one was a double yolk. I asked if that wouldn't do. Father said the double yolk egg shouldn't count - it wouldn't be any good. I begged him to let me try. I knew I had to wait twenty-one days to see if I was right. Every dry morning, when the broody hen didn't have dew on her feathers, I would turn and wet the eggs for her. Finally, I heard tapping in all the eggs but the double one. Last of all I heard tapping in the double egg, and it hatched out. Believe me - I do not lie -the chick had two heads and three legs. My father said, "It will never live." It didn't, of course, but it did live till evening!

The baker, Mr Wright from Polperro used to have a mule and trap. The mule was bad tempered - that's why we Cornish call mules "monthly tights". He'd kick up and batter the trap and bits. He came around two or three times a week.

We baked our own bread, though; we had a cloam oven. You couldn't beat the bread that it made. You'd take a bundle of furze sticks, light them, get them black, sweep them out and bang in the bread and yeast cake to cook. I can remember it now, with plenty of cream.

We had a boat and a canoe, solid mahogany, with brass trim, I think. Father said we could go down the river but NOT into the harbour. Well, before the war, we got very large Japanese ships in the harbour, much larger than now. One day I said to my sister, "Let's go across under the tugs to get some ice cream!" We did that - lovely - then waited our chance to come back. The next day Father came home from work raging. He never beat us, though Mother would sometimes give us a smack, like all mothers. He punished us by keeping our halfpenny back three or four weeks.

"How did you know?" we asked.

"Captain Wyatt told me."

I rowed up and down in a boat many times, rowed with my twin sister in many a Regatta, in a canoe or in the shovel race, etc. We won many times.

When World War I broke out, I was twelve. The Yanks were here then, officers staying at Fowey Hotel, which was then a convalescent home. They used to come up when the tide was up and have tea, scones and cream, jam, buttermilk at Mother's, all her own baking. They would bring up their posh fishing rods with flies. There used to be a pond above the sluice gates at Lombard Mills, quiet water, with hundreds of Rainbow trout (which didn't belong to us). The officers would come in without permission - well, they must have had a licence - and fish. We used a bit of cotton, a bent pin, and yellow dung worms we had dug out of the dung heap and caught loads of fish with that. The officers asked, "What bait are you using?"

"The Dung heap. Would you like some? We have half a jar left." They tried our worms and caught some too. After that we dug worms for them for the princely sum of 2/6d a time.

Most of the farm was hill. When we were fourteen it was war time, and we were told we had to till three acres of food. Our fields were all hill, they went as far as Porthpean House in one direction, and saw mills in the other. It was so hilly we had to do it all by hand. We did it, my sister and I, tilled and planted potatoes. We were presented with green armbands with red crowns on - war workers on the land, voluntary. But Father wouldn't let us wear the khaki trousers. We wore short skirts like now but not as long as yours.

The sawmill below was still working then; but it didn't belong to us though it was adjacent with the stream. At the sawmills they had a saw pit and wood was cut in planks for gates. We used to watch by the hour.

The Wesleyan minister, Mr. Canning, lived just one cottage up from Lombard Mills. On Sundays, before preaching at Highway, he would turn off the sluice gate. My husband wondered why, when the mill didn't work on Sundays. He watched while Mr. Canning picked up all the trout wriggling with no water in a bucket. My husband decided if the minister could do it, why not we? So after Mr. Canning went to chapel, my husband turned it off and also picked up a bucketful of Rainbow trout. He also saw a beautiful salmon peel. He brought it up in a shrimp net. I made all my own shrimp nets and rabbit nets to go rabbiting with ferret and dogs.

Mr Fortescue owned the other mill. Above the sawmill was all bramble and bracken. There, there was a cave, St. Wyllow's Cave. Once Arthur Quiller Couch came to us with two or three gentlemen. "Q" was a great friend of ours. He came here to us to find out about Fowey. We went out to the cave which was all overgrown. Father had to take a hook to cut the bramble and shovel because lots of rocks and things had fallen in. They could get in only about ten feet up at the back of the sawmill. I understand it was a tunnel which went all the way through to Polruan Castle where pirates used to come.

Father was Chairman for the Liberals for forty years. Isaac Foot was a prominent Liberal. I knew all the Foots - John, now Lord Caradon - they've all been here. Sister and I used to go canvassing. We used to stand at the door of Whitecross school, the polling station, seeing how many voted.

My husband and I were childhood sweethearts. We went to Whitecross School. Frank Mitchell, Skipper Mitchell, from Polruan, was our teacher. I passed for Grammar School, but Father couldn't pay the fees for both of us. So I was not allowed to go. It wasn't right, you know. I had to stay at school until I was fourteen, but after I had passed Standard 7 they couldn't teach me any more. So I was put to teaching the infants while the teacher sat back reading a book. She got the pay, not me.

Schools waste so much paper and all these days. We had boxes of silver sand. I would draw a cat or bird on the blackboard with chalk. The children would draw it with their finger in the sand. If it was wrong, they just shook the box and tried again. Then they progressed to slates.

I used to cycle from Pont to Polperro to my sister's house sixty years ago. At that time, if someone died, they would be left to lie in in the house, not in a mortuary as they do now. It was horses and carts then. There were no cars sixty years ago.

A child once asked his mother when a lady died, "Where has she gone?"

"To heaven, I hope," was the answer.

The child told the other children who asked him, "Where has she gone to?"
"To Heaven, I think."
"How did she get there?"
"By horse and cart, bloody fool! How else?"

BEATRICE JACOBS CRAPP
BORN IN 1903, SPEAKING IN 1983-1989

Mother was Eliza Lean, came from Lerryn to Polruan to work. Mother died when I was eight and my sister was ten. Father remarried, a widow with two children. Father was George Jacobs, Polruan born. Father's mother was a Menear. Father went to sea when he was young. And then he was on the ferry boat for a long time. He had thirty shillings a week on the ferryboat and we used to take that thirty shillings in pennies - he had it in pennies - down the butcher's shop to Mr Holton to change it. It was a penny, penny goin' to and fro.

He also did odd building jobs. Then he went to work at the docks, had an awful accident there - got jammed between bumpers - developed pneumonia, only lasted a week then died. He was a teetotaller, though. He was a Rechabite; so he never had no drink. We weren't brought up with drink. Never had no drink in our house.

I was born where Seymour Hicks lived in Fore Street. When I was two weeks old, we moved to Church Terrace, where Mother died. The house was tiny. The kitchen was as you went in. The stairs used to go up in the back kitchen where the furnace was and where we did our washing. We three girls slept in the back room in a big bed. The back room had a lean-to roof - later those cottages were modernized and now it has a nice flat roof. We didn't have a bathroom - toilets were out back, on main sewage but we had to fetch water to flush them. But Mother and my stepmother always kept us clean. We were always clean. Eddie, our brother, must have slept in a little bed in with my stepmother and father. My sister didn't stay long at home after my father's second marriage; she didn't get along with our new mother. We had a stove in the front room - a coal stove, the old range - every house had one. We must have cooked in the back kitchen I guess. Water came from taps just opposite St. Saviour's church gate.

Oh my, yes, it was hard work then. Stoves had to be cleaned, and we had boilers for washin'. You did it all and coped all right. I was grown up (when Dr Jay came with an electricity generator) We had candles and paraffin lamps, yes, brass ones, cleaned all up. Oil lamps were dangerous for children though. My boys were very fond of throwin' things in the fire, I might tell you, yes. Had to stop 'em.

Yeah well, the WI was allotments before. Private, you know, anybody that thought they'd like to do a bit of gardening. I don't know if they paid for it or not, but they always had it. Different men in the village, like. My husband was a lovely gardener, tilled gardens for people before he left school. Where we lived, we always had a garden; and then he'd till other people's gardens, you know, for them.

Many things were brought to the door - milk and vegetables. People came from Polperro. Carrie Charman's great grandfather came with horse and cart from Penpol. He sold apples, lovely turnips and all. He was Mr Rollings. He came Saturdays before dinner till after tea. Mrs Welsh's brother was Rollings and came with him. We went to the shop daily for our meat. Of course we picked blackberries in season. We could get everything we needed in Polruan, and Fowey of course.

Things were different then in Polruan. People helped each other. Children used to fetch water from the taps for the old people. We used to tap on the door to see if they wanted any errands done, any shopping fetched. I used to do all Mrs Cossentine's errands and fetch her bread Saturdays for three pence per week. She was a carpenter's wife - lovely people the Cossentines. They were the Chapel stewards and also had the Chapel collections - you could always get change there. Girls fetched little cans of beer and porter for uncle who worked coal bunkering. Young women used to do the washing for the old people too. Mother would come out of Chapel, go home and take some buns and tartlets up to one of the older men living alone. She wasn't well off but she thought he was poorer.

Up where Penhallow cafe is now, that was a grocer's shop - it was a post-office first, and then 'twas a grocer's shop. That was four post-offices there've been in Polruan, haven't there?. The post-office been in three places. But I remember the shop out there, Charlie Stephens, her son. And then where Mrs Hunking lives, a Mrs Hender lived there. And she used to sell bread there, lovely bread.

You remember Mrs Connor who lived out West Street? Well, course, we were the same age, went to school together. And after school we used to have to go over in little boat for the bread and bring back, to her mother on the quay. And she used to drop the oars in the boat and fall back. Used to frighten us, you know.

This was all fields out here (Greenbank). And then up the road, you know where Mr Frisby, well that was Mr Laiety's cowhouses, the last farm. Up further than the old reservoir, opposite the road. And my husband used to go up six o'clock every morning and go in Mr. Thomas's to milk the cows before he went to school. They left school when they was fourteen. There were about five farms up there. There was Libbys, you know, and Thomas and Kendall and Laiety. Townsend it was called. When we were children, we used to take milk around before school for the Libbys.

I tell you where we used to play a lot, in Church field I don't know how it is we were allowed to go in there, all around the church; but you see we only went in there to sit down. We used to do a lot of crocheting, knitting and that, sit down to do that, never went in to run around and tear the place up. Nothin' like that.

When we were older, we'd perhaps go down around in the evenin' and up around the hill and that - there wa'n' nothing much to do, really. Yes, we used to walk and course it was dark evenin's - you never was out very much in evenin's. We played games, snakes and ladders and that. See there was no television nor wireless nor nothin', really.

The trouble is you see, it was unfortunate for us cuz our mother died. I was eight and my sister was ten. I had a good mother, and she always used to take us to Chapel, you see. Well, my father married again eighteen months after. The doctor wanted me father to put us in one of these homes what they put in for children, but he wouldn't part with us. Sometimes I wonders if t'would have been better for us; we might have been more educated 'n' that. You don't know, do you? In they days we had to leave school when we were fourteen to go to work, never had the opportunities they have today.

There was Mrs. Dunn, Sylvia, she was called - she used to teach up there. And then there was Miss Mayow, Miss Mayow from Blisland. Very hard she was, but she was good teacher and you know she would catch hold your hand and smack your arm and you'd keep on pullin' it away. She was a great tall person, like gaunt, one of these tall woman; and she had great big bony hands, like. She used to wear nice red blouses and skirts. And of course, she used to always go home again to Blisland. She used to lodge over Moss Terrace, I think, with Mrs Hanson. And then, of course, she come up Friday dinner times all dressed up; so we knew that she was goin' home. So we knew that we'd be out of school early that afternoon.

I was very good at school. I was one of the best writers in the school, although I say it myself. And then I used to write little notes to Mr Billing, the schoolmaster, you know, about anything. And he come to me one day, and he said, "Mrs Crapp, what a lovely writer you are."

I said, "Well," I said, "I taught myself at school to write."

At school on St. George's Day we sang all national songs in the morning. In the afternoon there was tea and a bun. Vicar Caldecot would ask "Have ye had yer tea? Did ye salute the flag?"

Then, there was always regattas. Whit Monday there'd be the Jetties Regatta, they used to call it; and we used to go out in the boat and see the racin'. We always had a boat, a rowing boat, a nice big one. Yes we used to go up Cliff and have tea. My father always used to take us up there in the summer once, and down Polperro and Looe one day. Mr Libby up there had a horse 'n' wagonette, they had then. And then my father used to drive. And that was our little outing in the summer. We had friends down Polperro that kept one of the pubs down there. .

Mr. Libby's wagonette was like a trap with a hood over, like that, see. It held, oh, about four or five. And then they had one boxed in like a box. That's where people used to go fer to be married in that one, out to the Church. He was the first man with a car in the village.

There was an epidemic of diphtheria. Me daughter had it, the one that died, and Maureen Libby, that's me sister; and they were took to Liskeard. And some had polio. That hit the village too. One of Mrs Steele's daughters, she's proper cripple with it. She lives up Mixtow. She can't use one hand at all. You see, they've found such cures for things now it's wonderful i'n it, really. The doctor was afraid that I had mastoid cuz I had an awful bad ear. And you had to pay the doctors then.

No, I think that they did more home nursin', recipes and that - camphorated oil for the chest. Mr Stephens out West Street, that was the chemist shop. We used to drink sulphur, that was supposed to be good wan't it? Always had a jug full of sulphur 'n' that. Then you'd take a little drop in the mornin's. I suppose it was cleansing. A little wine glass full, you know. And then we used to have liquorice and bay leaves, for a cough; and that was in a jug, steamin'. And then you had a glass of that when you had a cough. And Angelica for inflammation wa'n' it. Laid on, like a poultice. Angelica, always grew angelica in the gardens. Also Father always made sloe wine - good if cold in the stomach. We also had elder tea for colds. For bad back we put nettles between two pieces of white cloth and applied it. It helped. Well, people goes to doctors for everything, don't they now? .

They used to have nice little concerts years ago, di' they, in the Sunday Schools and that? They had lovely winter concerts by the people in the village, you know. Yes, especially West Street Sunday School, where Miss Ransleigh's flats are. That was a lovely Sunday School out there. It was one big room and a gallery with a stage one end. You know Mr Toms, Jack Toms's father? Well, he used to bring somebody because he come from Taphouse, Mr Toms did. Then he was a blacksmith here; so they came here to live. But he used to bring a Mr King from up there, and he used to play the concertina and that. I remember the Hockens family, both Polruan and Fowey, were lovely singers, and Mrs Hunkin out West Street - Laurence's mother - was a singer, and I should imagine her husband, Norman, too. People came from away to them.

We had a lovely play up school, 'Cowler Helen'. A lovely play, that was. I was in that. I was a school girl, and I had lovely long hair.

Christmas was special. We always decorated, yes. I remember one year when our mother was livin', we had a Christmas tree in a pot of earth in the corner of the room decorated with shiny balls and the like; and we children upset the tree. We weren't allowed to have any more after that. But then, she didn't live really. With my stepmother we always had a tree, we always had Christmas. We hung up our stockin' - we never had a lot in it like they do today but we always had somethin', a penny, an orange 'n that. And there was always like a little china ornament with a few chocolates in. We always had a nice Christmas dinner, chicken or duck, and Christmas pudding and all, like today.

During the Christmas season, not Christmas day, people would be down the corner singing carols in the evenings. The men used to go around singin' then. People would go around singing carols in the village. And they'd congregate at the corner and sing most days ,but they don't do that now.

My husband thought a lot of Christmas. We always had a party for the children at Christmas, and the children always had stockings, and a nice dinner and pudding - goose etc.

We went to Fore Street Chapel. Sunday school ten am, Chapel eleven, Sunday school two, Chapel six. We had a lovely time at Sunday School, United Methodists. West Street were Wesleyans. Oh, it was lovely. I tell you who used to speak to us, Lloyd's father, Ernest Dunn. Yes, used to tell us funny stories. Told lovely stories. And hymns. Lovely hymns we had, same hymns as we singin' now really, Sankey hymns. We had reading the Bible and people tell you about Jesus and all that, you see. Oh yes, we loved Sunday School; and then after we'd go to Chapel, you see. Well, I mean to say, Sunday was Sunday in they days, wa'n it? There's no Sunday today, is there? They don't believe in the Sabbath.

We went out to Furze Park, Sunday afternoons sometimes. And then we used to go out with the children a lot. You see, they weren't very old then. Stanley Smith, do you remember Stanley Smith? Well, my sister worked for Stanley Smith's mother. And she was down there; and I had two children then, John and Margaret. And Mrs. Grundy used to say to my sister, "Now take Stanley and go up your sister's and go out Furze Park with un. So we used to take Stanley with us, you know, with my two children and my sister. There's a little lake down on the rocks. I never went down there with the children, I didn't. But my children used to go down there. Furze Park Pool that was called. A bit further on than Lady Ram's Rocks. I was always taken out Furze Park when I was little.

We used to go after chapel and sing on the corner. They had a little harmonium. Yeah. I used to enjoy that cause I love singing. Oh, I do, I enjoy singin'. Lovely. But they aren't allowed now, are they? They say they aren't allowed to sing at corners.

And we always had Whit Monday. Whitsun we always had our Anniversary. The two chapels got together for Anniversaries. West Street's was usually July. The Chapel was packed. We all dressed up - always had a new hat and dress. And we had a platform each side of the chapel and a lovely piece of wire netting down for flowers in front of the pulpit. There were recitations and singing, the boys one side and girls the other. And of course they used to do a repeat on Monday evenings. But over to Fowey 'twas the Regatta, and then they had doin's over Fowey in the evenings.

So I remember as if it was yesterday, we were in the vestry, and Mr Goldsworthy - that's Evelyn Slade's grandfather - he was the superintendent of the Sunday School. And he was there, and she was going up to play the organ, and she was turnin' over the pages. "Never ought to be here tonight. We could have gone over there. We could have come here tomorrow." she said, "We could have been over to Fowey tonight havin' a bit of fun." I remember that clear. She was lovely.

Well, when I left school, I went down the street to work, well, you know where the wool shop is, Jean's wool shop, (now Polruan Newsagent). Well, I worked there, not in the shop but in back doing the work. Mr. and Mrs. Bunny had a shop there, a grocery shop. And she used to make lovely cakes 'n' sell them and make their own ox puddings and meat and all that and sell. I never did no cooking. I used to do all the work, clean the stove. I did the washing, fetching the water from the court behind out of the taps there. The laundry had to be snowy white like Mrs. Jackson's who lived above. But she was a lovely kind person, Mrs. Bunny was, and they never done nothin' Sundays. But she'd always ask me to come down Sundays to lunch. I always went down there to lunch Sundays. Well, I think she thought, you see, I never had no mother. We had a step mother. I always went down Sundays.

Mrs. Parsons was next door. She wouldn't open no shop Sunday. Wa'n' never no shop open Sunday. Do all the shoppin' before. But the Catholics do, don't they? I think their Sunday ends dinner time do'n' it, mostly? Cause they go to church in the mornin'; then in the afternoon they do all sorts, don't they? But everybody please theirself what they do. I don't do it. I never done it. I'm not goin' to do it now.

I lived in when I worked at Mr. and Mrs. Kendalls (Haviland). When I got married, they gave me a chicken and some potatoes. Mr. Kendall was a lovely man. I used to take him up a cuppa tea. One day Mrs. Kendall said not to bother, that he'd soon be down for his tea; so I didn't take it up to him. When he came in later, he said, shaking his head, "Those that does all the work, them get nothin'."

We used to take tea out the fields, used to carry drinkin's out the fields when they were harvestin'. I took a kettle, a big kettle, and pasties and buns, you know. Mrs. Kendall made lovely pasties - meat, potato, turnip or bacon. Harvest buns - yeast with currents. Then they never had to stop. Right up the road in those fields up the road and the fields down here, Greenbank; this was all fields. They used to have the wagon then with the hay, you see, and I think we put it on the wagon and ride up in the wagon. When threshing we took lunch up to barn at Townsend, Mrs. Kendall and me. Fowl pies, chicken, boiled potatoes.

Mrs. Pearce is her daughter, but then she used to be away to school when I was up there. Yes, she went to college and that. And then they had a son. They had two sons, cuz one son farmed out to Triggabrowne. And then the other son, he went to the war, and he was gassed; so that he never got married, you see, he was home. He used to work on the farm. And then they used to have an old man called Tippett, that used to work on the farm, as well. Yeah, Tippett, he was called. lived down there in Fore Street in the cottages.

Used to be up early in the mornings and used to scald milk to make cream. I still do a little bit of it myself, you know. You wonders how you done it, though, really so much. I wasn't very tall, see. The stove was a great big black stove, you see. And then there'd be a great long kitchen and then a long dairy. You had to carry it all in there. These great hot pans of milk. I dunno how I did it. Cuz if it had upset, I should have scald to death, wouldn't I? The pans were white with two handles, yeah, white enamel pans with two handles. Lovely cream - you weren't allowed to hurry it up because wouldn't have no cream if you hurried it up.

Girls wouldn't put up with what we put up with. We never used to answer, we never used to answer. No, never. I know I wanted half a day to go in St. Austell to buy a hat an' that. "Whatever do you want to go in there for?"

I said, "Well..." I don't know if I went or not.

Mrs. Kendall was not bad because she was really delicate, you know. She was a little tiny woman, and she was delicate. And she only did the cookin'; she never done nothin' else. And then she'd have to go to bed after dinner. So I was in charge until four. I think she suffered in her stomach, you know.

Mr. Kendall was a big man. But then, he was kind, you know. They were nice, really, they were kind people. Kendalls lived out Pendower vicarage. Mr. Kendall's father was a vicar. I can't remember that.

They very good, very good livin'. And always went to Church Sunday mornings. Yeah, they were Church people. Never no swearin' or nothin' like that.

There was horse-racing. Several policemen came into tea at Mrs. Kendalls after - all Kendall friends in dining room. The racing was in a field out at the corner of the turning to Pont. Horses from Lanreath etc.

After I was married we lived at Corner (Quay Hill). Our first two children were born there. The house had a lovely staircase. Underneath was a shop belonging to Mrs. Libby, Percy's wife. Percy worked in Slade's yard. The shop sold fish and chips and ice cream and groceries. That was before the Tamblyns.

Later we moved to Rock Villa where we raised our children. There was a stove in the front room and a lovely white table by the window where I did my cooking. We had four children. Rock Villa was a slum when we went there. It had been Mr. Kinver's - not the publican. There was a lovely staircase going up in the house. In they days everyone had things grained.Well, when we had painted, old Mr. Welsh, a cabinet maker, came and grained it all. It was very damp though. I think I might have been happy there now if it hadn't been so damp. It belonged to Mr.

Kendall, Snowy Pearce's father. When we went there, there was a new toilet not long put in.

The garden and court were a disgrace, full of rubbish and rats. My husband was young, and there wasn't anything else to do like television now - we made a lovely garden. We used to have chickens and we used to keep pigs, yes. There was an orchard right in through where the garages are there, yeah, leading down through to Mr. Trulove's in Tinker's Hill..

We used to kill a pig at Christmas, and we had chicken. I used to have to do all that. We had the butcher to kill the pig. But we used to cure the meat, and I used to make nice tripe 'n ox puddin's 'n that - a few weeks' work that was. I learnt all that at the farm before I was married.

Oh, we used to have lovely skerrywigs, spider crabs, from out West Street from the Pills. Me mother-in-law would come over, and she'd say, "Now, I'll mind the children. Take the bucket 'n go out 'n get some skerrywinks". You used to get a bucketful for sixpence. We used to have to go down all those steps out there to their house. Never sees anything like that now, do you. Never sees a crab. Never sees a fish hardly over here, don't see no fish.

We used to make lovely watercress pasties. Lovely. Used to go out by Essa then, pick that. Well, watercress and parsley and chipple onions. And bacon and egg - make a lovely pie - bacon, egg, watercress and parsley and chipple onions.

Oh my yes, we was always up Carne Beach in the summer. Yes, and Mrs. Libby, my sister, and Mrs. Ward. Yes, and we used to go out Lantivet picnics, take water and sticks and all for a fire, walk out there, make pasties before we went, 'n' walk right out Lantivet. My husband never used to go with us cuz he was workin'. 'Twas my sister-in-law and I and the children. See, we had to mind the children. Well, you know where they are, don't you? And then we used to go right around the country with 'em sometimes. I used to love walkin'.

We always had time to help other people. Always used to help people. That white cottages that's up St Saviour's Terrace? Old people up there, used to go and help un. Do a bit of washin' for them, never got paid a lot.

There was an old gentleman called Mr. Quelch, he lived there. He was a recluse really. And he and my husband were very friendly, and he used to come down our place. But then me husband died, you see. And then he used to go to Fowey and come home perished with the cold and come in to me and have a hot cup of tea. He was a bit mean, you see. Then my husband died, and it was Christmas, and it was Boxing day. And I thought, now I better go up 'n' see if he wants any bread before they close or he won't have enough. He was in under the table and whether he upset the lamp or no I don' know. But he was burnt. And he left £19,000 to Barnardos, and we thought he was poor. Every Sunday when I come out of Chapel, my husband used to say, "Now before you take your coat off, my dear, what you going to take up to the old man, take up." And I'd take a bag of stuff, buns, all sorts. And he left all that money to Barnardos.

I was a member of the Women's Hour for fifty years. In the beginning the Women's Hour met at the old Church Sunday School. I went there when Mrs. Jouqhin first come to the first meetin, and Christine was a baby in arms. And she said, "I'd like to form a fellowship in the village." And she said that we needn't dress up. She said, "Don't dress up." And she said, "Come and bring your children." It was 1939, and that was that. And I went every week. I never stopped home from the Women's Hour only if I was ill. I never stopped home for anything. Faithful member I was, and I used to preside, you see, as well and do the tea.

ELLEN AND KEN HUNKING
BORN IN 1913 AND 1907, SPEAKING IN 1996

Granfer Tucker, my husband's granfer, was from Tresillian, came to Fowey for work in a little cart with his daughter, Adeline. There was no work in Tresillian. Adeline married George Hunkin. My father-in-law, George, was in the Naval Reserve down Penzance way and only came home for weekends or something.

My husband, Charlie's father, he was a Petty Officer in the Navy. That was the Naval Reserve. He used to walk from Looe, come here Monday, stay a week. walk home again end of the week. He was the gunner instructor. The fishermen was the Naval Reserve same as they are today. Polperro men used to walk to and fro. I don't know how many came to a time or whether they all come. Father used to stay the week, like. They would have stayed the week? I dunno, I doubt it, not from Polperro.

It used to be an armoury. Di'n' they stay up there? Fowey Armoury is the one that come from Battery. They used to lodge here cuz someone called Maslin used to come here as well. Maslin come here with father. He was the Chief Yeoman of the

81

signals in the Navy, he was. But whether he was retired when he took over the No. 11 of the Coastguard Houses, I dunno. See, he and Mr. Ricketts wasn't in the Coastguard; but he got in the Coastguards after he come.

They used to fire from the top of the hill. I can remember the people firing up from the path - you know the path up in underneath the garden as you walk out Peak - firing down against the stone wall. That's where the targets was. I can remember them there, lying on the grass firing at it. Yeah, the stone wall is still down there. The monument, that was on the hill, that was, further down than St. Saviour's Ruins, on the hill that other side. There was a piece there about six foot square. I should say there was three steps fer 'e to get up on top.

My father come here with the Battery. Oh yeah, that's why he come here. They wore much the same uniform as the Coastguards used to have. And the pilots was nearly always the same with their brass buttons or white buttons, peaked cap, white cap through the summer. The fishermen that was over Fowey would come cuz they would be under the same obligations as the rest of the fishermen, wouldn't they?

When they built the West Street Chapel, they called for lots of volunteer labour, of course. When it was built, Uncle Ernie climbed up with spikes in his shoes to attach the lightning conductor. It must have been an afterthought to put it up or something, because he climbed to the very top of the chapel with those spikes on his boots and fixed it up there. Everyone watched with mouths open. My mother didn't - she said she was in the bedroom on her knees!

When I was a boy in Polruan, you had plenty of freedom. You could go anywhere. I know that everybody used to be after 'e sometimes for pinching apples or something like that. Yes, apples in the gardens and around. Yeah. We never took em away, only one in the pocket only to eat. I mean, there wasn' no wilful damage done like they are today.

Father used to fetch the coal and all that sort of thing for Mother, di'n' 'e. We used to fetch the potatoes from out the farm. That was after when we was out Walk Terrace. I mean to say, we had the meadow fer we used to till potatoes - that's the place next door to Mr. Brickell's bungalow. We had a length of garden. There was four allotments there from Brickell's place to the road - 'twas the length from the Coastguard Station down to Hockens Lane, each piece. We used to till potatoes. The Coastguard had allotments - they had two gardens each, that stretched from down their double gates right around and come up to, what's 'e called?, Stuart's Cottage, see, on the bottom of the lane. Yeah, the Coastguards, they had a very big garden. I think back then nearly everybody wanted to be self-supporting in green stuff more than anything else. The only place that I know of that was allotments was Wherry Place - that field was allotments. And, course, there was Mr. Wherry. That's how 'e was called Wherry Place. He was a farmer. Well, he had a small holding up top, other side of the road from Lady Ram's.

We lived down in Well Court to start with. Then we went out to Walk Terrace. I can't give you the date exactly. But we was out in Walk Terrace when the war broke out in 1914 because I remember Mr. Steele coming down after Father one Sunday night. He had to go to Crystal Palace Monday morning. He went there, as far as I remember, as a writer to start with. Then he come back to Cardiff, from Cardiff to Cork, and then to Bodmin. He was recruited in to Bodmin. That was during the First World War.

I don't know how many there was, but there were several Territorial men - that was Fowey. They used to go over to Fowey Territorials. Several went there, I should say. Our Ernie - Ernie Hicks - Reggie Stone, Lawson Langmaid; you know, there were several. But they went on the Monday they was called. War broke out the Sunday night, and they was off the next day. Yeah, Capt'n Steele told the Coastguard. We never had no radio, no radio then. He got it over the telephone from the Naval people, I s'pose, see. I were seven year old. Well, we didn't know exactly what was happening, not really, see, cuz Father was not home all the time.

There was no papers in they days like there is today, was there? And there wasn't no wireless. The first I heard was when Marconi spoke from America. That was the first one we had. Ginger Taylor, Mr. Taylor, in Chapel Ruins he lived - we heard it from there. He opened the window, and we was there in the road.

At school we had a boy who was aboard 'HMS Cornwall', and he come to the school for Mr. Widlake, the headmaster. Whether he got him to come or whether he was some relation or no, I dunno. But he come there; and when we heard the airplanes, everybody would go outdoors and have a look. Cuz the first time that we seen any airplanes was during the war.

During the war we used to have little wood guns. I dunno who made them, somebody did. We used to, well, think that we was at war. We'd go out the Battery. They was homemade guns, just made from a bit of wood like, you know.

When the war ended, they had arches and that all built then. There was a good arch from the Russell Inn across West Street. They put 'em up at the same place as Jubilee - that's what I understood at that time. There was like a sports day.

At school Mr. Widlake was fairly strict, mind; but he was a master that knew his job. There was no doubt about that. Everybody respected him, yes. Because he taught we decimals and so the metric system, which wan't in the curriculum of the school. But I asked the second master why we had to learn the metric system. He said, "Yeah, but where do the boys go from here?"

"Well," I said, "they goes to sea, most of them."

He said, "Them going to sea, and they'm going on the continent. But if they don't know this, what are they going to do?" He taught them so they could communicate with the people across Europe. He was a wonderful master.

Mr. Widlake was a strict Wesleyan, wa'n't he? He was choir master out at the Wesleyans. Schoolmaster, choirmaster. He could play an organ, or he could preach the sermon. Wonderful!

But our best mate was Cornelius Pill. He'd always have a bit of fun with we when he'd hide away behind the stone wall, like, and just look out around and laugh and sneak off. Mr. Pill was a crabber, an', well, they used to do fishing, seine fishing they used to call it, like you know. He was always up Battery, see, watching for something, fish or something. The pilots used to have to go up top. Pilots, see, there was a dozen of they that used to be. Seven pilots and twelve Coastguards that used to be on duty all the time.

And the Tomlins, Ken and his father, they'd be up for to look for the boats that used to come. The little small vessels with cobbles, coal or stone or somethin' that they had to be worked out - they see un coming. They'd pull out to be the first one out there fer to get the job. Exciting life really. There was nearly always somebody up on the hill.

And down the Furze Park Pool. It's still there, yes, I expect so; nobody haven't altered that. Halfway out through Furze Park from Lady Ram's house out, about half way out. Ti'n't a very big pool, a little bit bigger than this room. I remember sailing little boats and that there.

Sunday was kept as a Sunday, a rest day. We always went to Chapel Sunday School first and back from the Sunday School, then in the Chapel and then dinner time. In the afternoon you might go out for a walk or anything.

If the weather was bad, we would play Ludo or cards or somethin' home, all hands but never on Sundays. All we lot was a good lot to play Snap. And do you remember the Magic Lantern? Charlie used to run it off out in the back kitchen - Magic Lantern. I remember him doing it fer us, blacking out the windows. I don't know, it was a battery or something. You had a little slide that you used to slide through, and he showed the light out through on the sheet. They'd have a white sheet or something so you could see. I don't know what it was run by -water in a saucer i'n't? Well, there must have been a fire in it cuz we had water. It could have been a little oil lamp, perhaps. I believe something to do like that. I know we always used to have water there. You used to buy they slides about that long and about an inch wide and slide that through. And that would be one little story.

While we was at school they used to get a conjuror or somethin' to come to Polruan, like, you know, a bit of magic. You must be able to remember the Pratleys. Yeah, they used to come around, little old clown Pratley, Otto Pratley? They used to come around doing something - just a little, well, concert party, wa'n it? I don't remember, but I remember them telling about it. I always thought he was a clown. We called him a clown, but he want no bigger than so big. But whether he did clowning, acting or anything, I don't know. I can't remember nothing about that. I only remembered his name, and I remember seeing pictures of him.

There were no street lights when I was a child. At Christmas almost everyone had a lovely Christmas tree of holly, and they could be seen from the street because people left open their curtains or shutters until ten o'clock, which was pub closing time. Trees were lit with small candles in tin candlesticks. I don't remember hearing of a tree catching alight ever.

On the Sunday before Christmas any man or lad with a voice came to this Chapel and sang beautiful carols. The choir stalls were packed full, the congregation singing the opening and closing hymns and one during the collection. The men did the rest - the singing was wonderful, a joy to hear.

Mr. Widlake, the Head Master of the Boys' Day School, was the organist. Mrs. Stone (Alice Wyatt) took over afterwards and has played the organ here for seventy years.

The Chapel was packed full. Sunday School forms were always brought out and placed the length of both aisles. The congregation were people of both Chapels and Church, and some who never went anywhere. All through the week leading up to the Christmas, men met on the Quay or the corner; and all joined in, sober or otherwise. There was no accompanist. They pitched the tune in their own key, and it was a delight to hear.

During the holidays several men went about in groups with their mandolins, tambourines, and mouth organs, dressed as minstrels. After three or four carols, doors were opened; and they were invited in and given hot ginger wine or hot cocoa. At some houses they were offered something stronger with the mince pies or slice of saffron cake. I never saw anything stronger than Stone's Ginger Wine, purchased from the grocer's, at our house, and we children had Eiffel Tower lemonade made from crystals from the same shop.

Several groups would walk into the country and visit the farms singing carols. They carried lanterns or jam jars with candles lit to see the words. Food and drink was always handed out. By the time they got back to Polruan, generally one thirty to two am, having drank cider and hot toddies, most were quite merry.

On Christmas Eve people who never went inside the Church at any other time joined hands and walked to Lanteglos Church for Midnight Mass. The church was always packed. Carols were sung as they walked there and back.

Christmas Eve was very exciting for us children when we hung up our stockings on the brass knobs of the beds. We always woke far too early, of course, to see what Santa had brought - one orange, one Clementine, nuts in the foot of father's stocking, a lovely rosy apple in the heel, a book to colour or paint with the box of crayons or water paints, a new white apron and maybe a toy. There was always a jar of sweets with Tom Smith's name on it. It was so exciting tipping out the contents on our parents' bed. They appeared to be as excited as we were.

Christmas Eve was, in the days of my childhood, the only time youngsters had new toys or games unless they were sick. The number and kind of toys etc. was altered according to how much work there had been during the year. But we were seven children, and all were treated alike in the value of things. And all were delighted and never wanted anything other than what was ours.

During the week, mostly the two or three days before the great day, women always made a huge batch of saffron cake. Some took their two pound tin of cake to the bake-house. I remember seeing six large tins of cakes brought back, all smelling

85

delicious. And they kept fresh and lasted all through the holidays, which was two weeks from school.

People exchanged their saffron buns and mince pies with friends and neighbours. We children took them about and were dared to eat any. It was supposed to be lucky, and every household who ate someone else's would be sure to have a happy month. Of course, if they were exchanged to twelve different families, a good year lay ahead.

All the family met for dinner on the twenty-fifth, if possible, at mid-day. 'Twas always farm turkey or goose. This was followed by a large wonderful Christmas pudding with silver three-penny pieces or a few charms in. And in the centre of the table was a tall cut glass bowl of sugar and another of gorgeous scalded cream. Ours was always collected from Mrs. Thomas's dairy before ten o'clock on Christmas Day, along with one pint of new milk and one quart of scald milk. That dairy was at Albany House, up Chapel Lane, where Mrs. Phyllis Turner resides now. We lived in Moss Terrace.

At tea time Aunties and Uncles who had no children came to our house and anyone else who was alone. During the afternoon we children played with our new toys and cracked nuts until we had to help prepare the tea. This was one day we were all willing to help - no one hid away that day. And what a spread! Always in the kitchen where the longest and largest table was. It was covered with a large white damask cloth, and the best china and cutlery was used. There were richer than usual saffron cake, mine pies, cold sandwiches, a large bowl of fruit salad, a trifle, and white bread and butter cut from a shop loaf for a treat. Brown cake and a cracker each to pull; so we all wore paper hats.

After the cups and plates was washed and put back in the glass cupboards, we were allowed to go upstairs in the best drawing room and sing carols. We were all on our best behaviour; so we could have a treat. This was to stay up for supper when we had cocoa and cold drinks, some cold turkey, ham, meat patties and any cold roast potatoes that were left. Ten o'clock we were off to bed, tired and happy, one more wonderful Christmas night and day over.

Well, I left the school the same time as Mr. Widlake. When he retired, I retired. Yeah, I stayed, performed with 'em when they was out on strike. I know that they wouldn't let the new Headmaster, Tipping, land on the quay. He had to go down Dunns yard for to get out of the boat.

Yeah, 'twas a pity that Mr. Roberts couldn't have took the school, really, cuz he was a good master. Cuz, not every Friday, but once a month - we used to go paper chasing. A couple boys would go off with their haversack full up with little bits of paper, what was cut up from an old exercise book, and lay a trail somewhere; and the rest of us would have to chase un, find where he was.

And Skipper Widlake would say, "Back here by twenty to four," for prayers fer to shut the school. We used to stay out in First Hill 'n look at the Fowey clock. And we'd wait till quarter to four. We never go back to school. But Mr. Roberts say at twenty to four you be here at school, and they would all be back. He would, well, I don't know, he would mix with the boys different. And he reminds me of, as I remember, in the sort of manner as John Robert Shaw. I don't know if it's right or no. He was very good. But we liked him as a master anyway. If you wanted to know something, you could go and talk to him; and he would explain anything to you, like I said.

I walked with him one time at a bell ringers' outing from out here. I forget where 'twas, down somewhere, where he was to. And the vicar give me the address of Mr. Roberts. We went down there. He was down there with two others sitting on the bridge. I said to Horace Tyro, "Caw, look who's down here on the bridge then," as we was coming away down with the car.

"God," he said, "That's the schoolmaster." Well, we got out an' spoke an' stayed fer a while. He was the captain in the tower. The bell used to ring there in the tower. He was the choirmaster 'n used to play the organ in the church.

There i'n't the people here now, see, than there was at that time. I don't know how many girls that was there, but I can remember the little blackboard - 109 boys. Well, I can remember 102 girls. Well, that was the infants, as well. Infants was boys and girls. And then they went over to the Boys' School when they was seven. But the two schools together was always reckoned up, and we had, I can remember, 102 of them. So that's 300 children nearly, see - 250 kids. They've got several in the school now, havn' they, more over there now than they've had for a bit. Well, and when I left, it was only 50 something - I think it was 59 - that was the boys. So there you are. When they opened up the Secondary Modern School, of course, you see that done away with a good many.

I wouldn't say it was any better, because we had more tradesmen in they days than we had scholars, di'n' we. Yes, I mean to say, it was the time of the life we was living in then. Everybody, the young men and the young women, went. They went over to Fowey and learned their trade as dressmakers and served behind the counter. And the men went somewhere and served their time, either on the farm or, you know. But now, you see, there's none of that, is there? Now everybody got to get everything with their mind in it. Since they put in the Secondary Modern School, they lost the use of their hands and that.

Well, yes and no. I think the point of that is, when the apprentices had that amount of money, they had to have a third of whatever the men was getting. Well, I mean to say, you couldn't charge the boy's wages fer against the customer. Because, I mean, he wasn't doin' anything, not for the first twelve months. I think that was what spoiled the employers for to take on apprentices.

You never used to have to pass exams then, did 'e, like they all got to now? Well, I mean to say, the point was if you didn't know it, there wasn't anybody that wanted 'e, was there, for work. If you couldn't do your job, that was that. You wasn't wanted. Yes, I was one of the lucky ones, that's all. Very good tutors, that's all I can say. I know I was always labelled as one of the best apprentices in the harbour here.

Parke Lees started Fowey Direct Building Company. Yeah, that was the beginning of it. We built that house out Tower Park for him. He had a nice house built there, too.

Father always asked what I wanted to do when I left school; he said it several times. I said, "Well, I should like to be a carpenter." I think that could have been through the carpentry class over Fowey, see, going to school. Might be, I don't know. Couldn't say whether that influenced me or no, but I always fancied that I liked the woodwork, you know. I went with Mr. Cossentine; he and his father worked here in Polruan. I went with him fer about, oh I dunno, about two months, I suppose; and he never had nothing to do. So he said, "I'm very sorry, but I sha'n't want 'e any more."

So Mr. Barnecutt, from Churchtown, he always come to Wesleyan chapel. And of course I used to go to Chapel every Sunday all the same. So he said - we was outside talkin' about it - so he said, "You can come out with me tomorrow, if you minded."

So I said, "All right, I'll be out." So I went out there fer, I dunno, twelve months nearly, I suppose. And Charlie Pearn come to Moss Terrace and said that they wanted a mason's labourer over Fowey if I would like to go. So I went along with them, and they built the house end of St Fimbarrus, that was Mr. Hooper's. But I wa'n't there not - I think 'twas about three weeks - and he said, "Oh, the house that we was hopin' that we was goin to help to build, somebody else has got to it and had put in a lower tender than we did fer it." And that was that.

And I went out next week with Mr. Barnecutt again. Farm work, yeah. Charlie Pearn was workin' for Jimmy Andrews. And Father was workin down Slade's Yard then; and he said, "I think Mr. Slade is going to have a fair little bit of work, bit of wood work." So he said, "When you goes down the street, you wants to go in and see un."

So I went in to see him, and he said, "Well, the 'Jane Banks' have run into Dover pier, and there's a brave bit of work." So he said, "Towards the end of the week, the 'Gallant' is goin' up 'n tow 'er down." So then he said, "I'll let 'e know whether. It'll be in about a fortnight." He told father fer me to call in an see un; so I went down and seen un. And I started the Monday week down in Slade's Yard. I was down there fer, oh, six months, six weeks. And then went back to Churchtown again. Yes, the job was finished. He never had no more work for me cuz he had, I s'pose, about a dozen or more men down there workin' then.

Then Father got the job fer me to go fer to learn me trade. Now they do that in the schools; but then it was up to you fer what you got, I think. But there was plenty of work then. See, that was 1923 when I started. What 'e call, things begun to pick up then, yes. Until the '30s, see.

Well, the vessels wa'n' here for the woodwork to be on. You see, there was two yards, you see, - Heller's yard that used to be up Caffa Pill and Slade's Yard here. Cuz they had the dock down where Newquay Docks is. That's why it's called Newquay Docks. Butson went with Mr. Watty, di'n' un; but they was on smaller boats. Slade's yard 'n Heller's yard, I mean, they was more repairs in my time. I mean to say, they never built no vessels, not in my time.

Grandfather's old blacksmith's shop was down in Joe Shea's yard outside the Grey House, other side of Waterfront. You know there's a small walk, say from Dunn's yard to Bunt's yard in there. Well, that's where it was to. And his shop was down there. I mean, the fireplace was there for years and years.

Where Polmarine is, the yard was there, because Mr. Burns, he used to keep Miss Wheeler's, all her sails and small boats. And that not in Bunt's side but the next one, down over the steps, White Rabbits. Well, that was a store. Yeah, we used to go over there when I was down Well Court, with Mr. Burns in the evenin's, like, you know, fer to pass away the time with the boats an' that.

Miss Wheeler she had the 'Saucy Nell'. Miss Wheeler was a Fowey lady. Granfer Hunkin used to sail with she, di'n um, Granfer Hunkin? I think so. Charlie's grandfather.

Yeah, the blacksmith's shop, 'twasn't very big. But, then, he still had the little yard at the front there that he could put all the - I mean, most of the blacksmithin' then was attached to the vessels that they was doing, see. The Slades had their own blacksmith's shop, see. The only one I can remember was Charlie Toms. Must have had someone before that. Must have been somebody. But then, I don't know. I don't remember. Cuz Uncle Phil, you see, when he was a lad, he was out Pont, wa'n't he, learning as a blacksmith. Langmaids, where Robin Rollings lived, near the corner at Watergate. Uncle Phil went out there to learn blacksmithin'. Yeah, wa'n' that so. But they was called Reynolds. It was before the Langmaids got there. So there was one out there. But that must have been more farmer blacksmithing, yeah that was. Then he went in the dockyard, di'n he? Then the war come.

There was a blacksmith in the back of the post office. 'Twas there. I can remember the blacksmith shop there, but I don't remember anybody there workin'. I know they used to say that the blacksmith there could pick up the vessel's anchor down Quay and take un up there, carry un up there.

There were no regattas when I was a boy cuz the war was on. Between the wars I wouldn't say there was many visitors that come here at all. I remember looking out from Moss Terrace with glasses and seeing all the ladies with long dresses come over the Yacht Club. And they always had a band there, di'n um. Oh, what's it called, come from Bodmin? Cornwall Light Infantry? Or Marines? I remember that though. But 'twas ordinary little pulling boats, kind of, that rowed, wa'n' it. Oh yeah, and they used to have a shovel race. But that was in my time. I mean, I don't know about how early that was.

They was four regattas here, wa'n't there. You had Jetty Regatta, Bodinnick Regatta, Fowey Regatta, Polruan Regatta here through the year. The Shovel Race 'd be in all of em. 'Twas an ordinary boat that you'd have. There was half a dozen of 'e in there with a shovel, the kind of shovels that they use at the jetties. Well, you call it a spade. 'Twa'n't a shovel, but they called it a shovel, like. And Fowey Regatta was later than 'tis now, and I believe Polruan Regatta was in August, wa'n it? Yeah, well, it used to be August Bank Holiday, Polruan Regatta, exactly the same as Looe.

Fowey Regatta, I can remember it was September. Yeah, I think that that was owing to the different places that where the yachts was to fer to race. They used to come down from up Cowes right down through, you know. And I think Fowey Regatta was after Falmouth, whatever date there was. Course, the Yacht Club arranged it all, di'n they? Tuesday was the Yacht Club Regatta, 'n Wednesday was Fowey Regatta wa'n it - with the carnival and that? It was all in Fowey Regatta week, but they used to reckon that Tuesday was more sailing than anything. Could be five o'clock before there was any pulling. Even when they come up with the four-oared boats, that was always late, wa'n it? Always wait till the sailing was all finished.

What 'e call Jetty Regatta was always Whit Monday. They used to start at the jetties and come down through the harbour and right out the mark out to Castle mostly for Fowey Regatta. But they never used to come down no more than to Fowey Quay for Jetty Regatta. Didn't Bodinnick Regatta turn into the Jetty Regatta after? I don't know whether they amalgamated or no. I don't think that they had the two the same, you know. I think when Bodinnick couldn't get any more to do it, the Jetty and they turned together.

Mr. Harvey was looking after the Sardine factory at Brazen Island. They had finished doing the salting in the pilchards, but he was still looking after it before Hobbs and Lindsey took over down Brazen Island, which they had. When they took over, they was on bunkerin' steamers an that with steam coal. They used to have a load of coal in 'n' dump it in the yard, and they had these two barges from up in the Thames. They used to go and bunker the ships with the coal. Mr. Harvey used to live on the end of Elm Terrace - Elm Cottages. He was a decent bloke. You would say the children looked up to him more than anything else. He was a gentleman, put it that way. His daughter was Mrs. Elliot, known later as Granny Elliot, mother to Gordon.

People had to walk to visit places then. Well, that was nearly the only way that you could go unless you had a pony and trap. There was two here in Polruan. Old Mr. Libby, Sam Libby? Mr. Libby had a trap and, what 'e call, Officer Crapp and Capt'n Bill Stone. But that was for their work though. They had a jingle fer to let out as well, cuz, what 'e call, Mr. Langmaid, used to drive, Napper's father. Yes, he looked after the shop fer Varcoe, down on the corner. That's right. He had a son called Willie Langmaid. He used to drive the pony and trap fer Capt'n Stone, the coal merchant. And then they come up the street where the Penhallow Cafe is, and she had a shop in there, di'n she, Mrs. Langmaid.

They didn't travel, not to that extent, not then. But I can remember going to Looe in a pony and trap. Yeah, years ago, down there, Looe Regatta, we used to. But we used to go down 'n see Aunt Margaret there in the pony and trap, 'n I remember the horse stopped out to Pelynt. As you come up around from Looe, you either go up there or come this way, don't you, to Fowey. Well, on the corner there was a - I don't know if 'e's still there or no - a big trough where the horses stopped. Well, we got nearly to it - he knew the water trough was there, you know. I can remember that. I don't know whether you was with us or no. But we'd been down to see Aunt Margaret.

CLAUDE RICHARDS
BORN IN 1911, SPEAKING IN 1996

I used to hear about when certain people was holdin' crab pots, they would pick up a line of contraband. Yeah, and drop 'em and lay 'em down and make it look as though it was lobster pots. And on one occasion there was two brothers and a son of one of the brothers. They picked up this, and they brought it in. And on the way to the Revenue Cutter, when they was seized and took alongside, he said, "We were comin' alongside, Sir, to give you this. We picked it up," they said. But they didn't take any notice of that. They were immediately impressed into the King's service, the Navy, and they were shipped across. I think the boy was on a different ship than the others, and this ship went down to Spain, and the other two was on the French coast. Apparently, if you were caught with any kind of contraband, there was no excuse whatever; and you was automatically put into the King's service. And once aboard one of them ships, you was lucky if you ever come out.

Yeah, I used to hear about 'em. You see, it started off with - we were playing marbles. You know where the car park is. That was where the Boys' School was, and we were outside of there playing marbles. And Edward Puckey won marbles from me; so I was pickin' up that one and felt a thud in the back. And it was Mr. Bray's milk cart, pony and trap. And the wheels had rubber tyres - rubber wheels - and it struck me. I was sick and taken home. Dr. King come to Polruan. And he still had his Navy uniform, but his rings was taken off. And he said, "Bruised the back of his heart, and he mustn't go up the hill again." So I wasn't allowed to go up over the hill to go to school again.

And then Edward Puckey and Jack Turner and me brother and Horace Tyro said, "But we can give him a piggyback up."

"That won't do."

"Well, we can give him a piggyback up, and then he can do his lessons. And when we'm out playin' football, he needn't join us. He can watch us."

Well, I wa'n't allowed to do that. So I never went to school from the age of - I think I was about seven or eight years old. I never went to school again. So what little education I had was what I had home. But I haven't found it hampered me a great deal. Because I've always been in work, and I've always had very good jobs.

My brother and I used to go down to the bake-house and get a sack of ships' biscuits. The biscuits had been made there and put up over to dry. They were so hard it took hours of soaking before you could get your teeth near them. One boy would take the end of the sack over his shoulder, the other two of us would each help by taking a corner; and we'd carry it down to the boat, then row with it out to one of the ships. In return, they would give us a biscuit or two with, perhaps, a drink of tea or coffee; and we'd stay and have that. After a while, the Mate would come along and say it was time for us to leave.

We were glad of times like that, though. My father didn't have too good a time of it. It wasn't his fault. But when I hear folks say that back then they always had plenty to eat, I don't know. I think they went a bit hungry at times, too.

And my first job at fourteen. Like all the others from Polruan, or most of the others, I wanted to go to sea. Against my parents' wish - my father was a bootmaker; he had a little shop in Fowey - I joined the 'Lydia Cardell', a barquentine, Fowey vessel, under Capt Baynham of Charlestown. And there was two chaps on her. They were engaged to Polruan girls; the bo'sun and the AB and then meself on deck and the cook - he was an old skipper hisself. And they used to teach me all sorts of things about the sea.

And I know one time we loaded clay in Penryn. We discharged coal in Falmouth and went up river to Penryn and loaded clay. We was bound to Aberdeen where it was going to be shipped in the barges and go to the factories. And then we were going to load coal for Penzance. And I remember we was goin' up, and it just must have been about the first or second trip up that way I'd been. No wind but she was rollin' like hell. But I wasn't feelin' seasick. And I was really on the top of the world. And the ship kept twistin'. And my mate, Cap'n Charlie, he said to me, "Take it, t-take the wheel, boy, t-t-take the wheel, boy!" He used to catch his words you see.

And I said, "Yes." I thought I was some big then. I was bigger than the foremast of the ship. I had the wheel, and he was smokin' his pipe.

And he said to me, "Here, I'll take the wheel. Th-th-that side. I don't know what time it was at night and the moon. I walked up. "Don't go past the galley, mind. You'll break in the fo'c's'le."

So I walked up an' back again. Done it again. I come back. "There's a light flashin' over there."

"N-n-no, it's not a light flashin'. It's a light bearin'."

I said, "Oh."

"Y-y-y go again, then."

Come back. I says, "There's a light bearin'?"

"Y-y-y-ya know the ship is stealin'. And you know how many points she is away from the head of the ship. Now you know, go up again, and tell me a-what." I had to do it again. And the third time he said, "G-g-g-good boy, good boy." So he said.

I said, "What light is it, Capt Jory?"

"That would be the Spern, the Spern lightship, yes. Now, I'll tell you. First the Dudgeon, that's the one we just passed, Lightship. Then the Spern. Withensea light is in the town. See boy, you see, then, the ray go over. You see the roofs of the houses shinin'. Now,

> Withersea light in the town.
> Flamborough light comes next in turn.
> But Fylie light is in the bight,
> And Whitby light is burnin' bright."

He was a nice old chap. But he wasn't scared of whippin' his arm across your ear if you didn't do what he told 'e.

And it wasn't long after that before the skipper, Capt Baynham, come up on deck and he looked and he said, "You go up. Tell that Scotchman to come back. So I went up, and I told the chap. And the chap went and took over, and I went to sleep.

I was only fourteen, but I wasn' the only one who went at that age. You see, Bill Allen, Iris Allen's father, Eileen's husband, he was only fourteen when he went to sea. A lot of them was that age. But some of them was ex-grammar school, and some of them was standard secondary school. And they all finished up as Master Mariners, captains of ships. One of them Cap'n Holton, he was skipper in the P & O line.

Well, after two years, "Lydia Cardell" went into Polruan Quay with coal. And we got in there about four in the afternoon. And by the time we got the hatches off, and got everything ready for unloading, had tea, and I cleaned meself up - I had a wash that day - I went aft. And Capt Baynham and me mates was talkin' and havin' a smoke. "What ye want, boy?"

I said, "I want to go ashore for an hour."

"I'll find a job fer 'e."

"No, I want to go ashore 'n see my mother and father." Capt. Baynham looked at me, the glasses down over the point of his nose cause he was readin' the paper.

He said, "Mind you'm back here before ten o'clock, mind."

I said, "Yes I'll be back before ten, Capt'n." I went home; and much to my disgust, I was told I had to leave the ship and go to work for Mr. Toms. So I had to leave the ship an' go to work for Mr. Toms, that's Charlie, Jack's father. He was a blacksmith and an engineer; so I had to go to work for him. Four years.

Jack had left Grammar School. And Charlie said to me, "Yeer, Jack is leavin' grammar school. I shan't want you any more. There's not enough work here for everybody."

So I went on the same ship back again. She had an engine put in her then, 'Elsa Craig', hundred horsepower. And I went back on her as an engineer/deck hand. I really enjoyed it, lovely. I didn't get seasick Then I went herrin' drivin' on a Mevagissey boat called the 'Gypsy', belongin' to the Barberry family. And we had some very exciting times at sea. But other 'n that 'twas all right. Didn't get much money. I think I made about £5 a month. Plenty of fish to eat and, of course, born in March, a python (Pisces) I don't like fish, not to eat. But I was glad to eat it because there was nothin' else, was all boiled. Polruan men used to do all right.

I used to go down in the - not the old linney what you know - but the older one. He was very low. And there was old skippers sittin' around. And I'd go down. And there was one Capt Jack Richards -he was no relation to me-, and Cap'n Bill Climo. I said, "Look, I'm one of them, you see. If you please, sir, can I come in the cabin?" And I wouldn't have a 'Yes' but have a finger pointed. When I'd sit down, I had a finger put across his mouth. And I sat down. I wouldn't dare speak. And they'd be there talkin' about their sea experience and different things that happened.

And I heard Cap'n Bill Climo, he said about the famous murder case in Fowey of the Jew and the pub. And one - might have been a couple days after - he was there. And I said, "Mornin', sir."

"Mmmm." Pointed to the seat. So I said, "That Jew that was. Was he stayin' in the Lugger?

"No," he said, "The pub that he was stayin' in stood where war memorial is now."

I said, "Oh?"

And Captain Climo used to say, "In them days there was only a very, very narrow street. And a pack horse could go through, but you couldn't get anything with wheels. And Rashleigh, when he built it, they hadn't finished all the buildings. And the roadway up was only for a pack horse. Course," he said, "the pack horses used to go along and go up the other way." You know where Sideways is, up Bull Hill? Well, there was no steps there. That was the main road before the main street was built. Rashleigh done all that work. I understand from these old men that Rashleigh, John Rashleigh, he had two ships the 'Christopher' and the 'Florence'.

95

And the Black Prince. And Rashleigh asked the Black Prince for permission to build a wharf that his ship could lay alongside. And you know the Riverside Hotel and the original ferry slip. And at the end of the ferry slip there's a little wall that sort of runned in a house built there now. That's the quay that Rashleigh built at first. And the Black Prince told him that if he sent one of his ships to Florence - I'm sorry, Bordeaux - and brought home a load of wine, he could have permission to build where he like. So John Rashleigh, he built the quays all the way down and dug away and made the streets, Fore Street, etc. And when you come down to Albert Quay, where the Toyne and Carter ship office used to be, there was an island. So he dug the island away, and the stone was used in buildin' what we call Albert Quay and further down.

But the merchant that had built and lived in Noahs Ark, he complained because his ship couldn't get in to alongside of his door; so his ships used to go right up beside of the Noah's Ark. Well, when Rashleigh dug the island and built the wall, so he was told by the Black Prince if he didn't like it, the entrance of the harbour was down there. And so there was no more said about it. Just fancy.

And I remember - I can't give you the correct date, but I think it 1937 - I didn't have anything to do. And fishin' was bad; so I couldn't go on the herrin' drifter. So I took a job with Berrill's Coal yard, deliverin' coal. And the pipes laying new water mains in the street. And outside of Julians - 'tin't Julians now; its Spar, i'n it - and John Eaton's cafe - outside of that, and they were diggin' down they come across lovely bright sand. And the chap that was on the lorry, Charlie Carne. I said, "You know, Charlie, I been told that John Rashleigh dug away a big island from here rock and built it. And I said, "That's the sand."

He said, "That's what it looks like." And that was done all the way down.

Like Polruan ferry, when the ferry was going. The old skippers in the linney used to tell me that in 1515, when the King come to Polruan, he stayed in the beautiful manor house, new manor house of Lord Mayow - the fish 'n chips shop when you knew it. And he was so impressed by the way that Polruan people was lookin' after his archers on board the ship as they were going to Ireland and the Netherlands. And they fed them on fish. And they made up clothes fer 'em. And the monks that lived out to Pont and the ones who lived down St. Saviour's church on the hill, they got tin out of the streams; and they made shields. And some of the archers was able to go into battle with the shields. And then they found that if you had leather and the leather was dry, the arrow didn't penetrate the shield. And so they made shields out of that.

And the king gave sanction that Polruan could make walk ways - pathways, I suppose that means - into streets. West Street - West Street was always known as the Walk -, and East Street and South Street - Fore Street now - And that was all made.

And Polruan Quay was formed and started. But Polruan quay was built in several different sections because, when a ship was out abroad, she would be comin' home in ballast. And she would bring home sand or gravel. And then they would build a piece by the time the ship got back; so that her ballast was put in to fill up. And so Polruan Quay would be like a egg box, really, if you could lift the top off.

And Polruan Ferry, there was a man. The King gave the ferry rights to the ferry-man. And I can't think of his name, but he sent the ferry rights down. And when this man finished with the ferry, it was to go to the Fortescue Estate. And nobody dared run against it, the franchise.

And so a man thought he'd like to stay home from sea. And he had a boat built. In them days a fifteen foot rowin' boat with a pair of paddles used to cost £9, yeah. I don't know, somewhere around a thousand now, I think. And this man did the ferry. And the proprietress was Mrs. Jane Hill, the wife of Captain William Hill. And she told the man that he's to stop runnin' against her ferry. "No," he said, "I ain' goin' to stop; I'm goin' to do it. I'm not going back to sea."

So it led to a court case. And the man was told that if he took one person, even one of his family, from Polruan to Fowey, landing anywhere in Fowey, he would be put in prison and his boat sold. But as he was a family man, they'd let him off with a caution.

I do remember about 1922 the ferry was sold, and the new operators were Polruan men. And they done away with the rowin' boat. And they had another motor boat built, which meant they had two motor boats. And it was a motorized ferry; so they put the fare from the penny return to a penny each way. And people wouldn't pay. So the ferry used to - they used to go around to collect fares, and they wouldn't pay at Whitehouse. So they would stop the engine until they did pay.

I remember when I was the lifeboat mechanic; and I had a bad illness, pneumonia. And the lifeboat I was in was the Humber lifeboat, 'Yorkshire'. And I couldn't sail her; so I was discharged on grounds of health reasons. I didn't know what to do; so I worked for Jack Toms for a while. And then Jack didn't have much work.

And William John Tomlin was the night ferry - that's Kenny, Roy's father. And Bill Stone said to me about takin' it on, and I said, "Yes, I will." So I took the night ferry on, and I had it for twenty years. I had my first boat, 'Rosemary'. She was built over Toms's. And then I had another one built. But I found that the ferry was peculiar, really, because you'd be down there sometimes about four or five hours; and you'd bring home about seven or eight people. And you'd be down there perhaps two or three evenings after, and you would have people in your boat every trip. But my fare wasn't penny return.

When I first took the ferry over, it was sixpence old money; so I can tell you runnin' at sixpence. And then the ferry fare was rose, and you were not allowed to run for the same price as the day ferry. You wa'n't allowed to do that - you had to charge more. So their fare went up to eight pence, and mine went up to ten pence, and Mondays it was two shillin'. There used to be a lot of grumbles; and I said, "Look, I can't help it. I'm not allowed to run for the same price as the day ferry."

And then I had orders that my boat had to be Ministry of Transport, Board of Trade; and I would have to go before the Board and be tested. So I was going to have to go to the Harbour Office, and I thought, "Oh well".

And my brother said to me, "Take yer papers over with 'e." So I took me papers over from the 'Lydia Cardell', and from another one I went on for a while and me papers from the Life Boat Institution and me papers from the herrin' drifter.

So I said, "I got these."

"Fold em up, and put it in your pocket, Mr Richards. Thank you for comin' over. You'll have your certificate posted to you in a few days." They never asked me one question. They wanted to verify that I'd been on the water. And so that was all right. So, like I said, I had the ferry for twenty years.

And when I went up to Brampton and had the heart operation, the ferry company done the ferry for me. And when I got back, "Thank Christ you'm back! Oh," they said, "I wouldn't have this."

I've often started on the ferry at half-past seven in the evenin' and got home the next mornin' between half-past six n' seven, yeah, many a time. And sometimes when it been bad weather and the quay been under water, I got home about then; and Polruan Ferry Company would come down to the quay. And they would get aboard of my boat, and they'd take my boat and do the first two or three hours as the tide would go back a bit. "She's better to handle, better engine than what we got."

I said, "I should hope so." You see, with the experience of the both sides, the boat and the engine, I was able to keep me engine in first class condition and me boat. And, of course, Bill Barberry, he was a expert boatbuilder. And we were friends for years; so I used to be with Bill when he was buildin' boats, not workin' for him, just like friends together. So I had a good idea on boat repairs. So a lot of things I used a do meself.

Anyhow, I would often put from half-past seven in the evenin', say twelve hours for about ten shillings. That's not bad. Every night about eleven o'clock I would bring Russell Tamblyn back - he was barman at the Riverside Hotel. Then there was a man from the Fowey Hotel, Albert Sanford. Then there was four girls used to come home; two from the Quayhouse Hotel, one from the Rockside Hotel. And they used to come home. I'd pick 'em up at the Riverside Slipway. Or if 'twas very bad weather, I'd pick em up at Fowey Quay. They always used to know where I'd be going cause they knew the weather conditions as well as I did, they girls.

And then I was sorry, really, when I become the age that I had to finish. I wouldn't have finished quite so quick because bein' - I never tasted alcohol in my life nor tobacco. And I think that was the reason why I got over my heart operations so well. And I would like to have stayed on the ferry for several years longer, but the insurance wouldn't take me. And the board of Trade said "No, we don't have nobody of your age."

An' I said, It won't be long till you'm cut, Lakeman."

And he said, "A matter of fact," he said, I've only got about a few weeks to go."

I used to have some fun on the ferry. I remember one night it was comin' somewhere about the middle of August, and I put a man and a woman on board of their little yacht. They had some kind of business in St Austell, and I often used to pick 'em up, put 'em ashore, or put 'em aboard. Anyhow, Mr. Toms used to look out fer the yacht fer 'em cause he had lots o' yachts on his books that he looked after. And comin' across, another man - I believe he was called Hunter - he was a architect from Polperro, and he'd been over Fowey to dinner. He said, "Claudie, there's someone up there," he said, "cryin'."

"Well," I said, "Will 'e come up with me?"

"Yeah." So we went up; and this was the girl, the woman that I put on board the yacht 'bout a hour before. And her husband had fallen overboard.

So I said to im, "Will 'e?"

"He said, "Yeah." So we went down, and we put the searchlight on, and we was lookin'. We didn't find un; so we got down the mouth of the harbour. It was light. He said, "Look!" And there was the man. And he fell overboard. And he had a rubber mattress, and he flung his arms around the rubber mattress which kept him afloat. And he was down off Donald Point, you know, Fowey Castle, and the point runs out. And, a course, we picked him up and took him back aboard.

And another time it was Fowey Regatta night, half-past two, three in the mornin'. A man come down, an he was well, well the worse for drink. He had a lovely suit on and a yachting cap with a badge 'n you would have thought that he was the Lord I am. "Take me to my yacht."

I said, "Yeah, where is she? Look," I said, "there's heaps of yachts in the harbour. So you tell me which one it is."

"Just inside the tug."

I said, "All right." So I said, "Well, that's a French yacht there."

So he said, "Damned idiot! That's my yacht."

"I don't think so."

"Don't you think I know my yacht? I'm not a damned Cornish idiot."

So I said, "No." So I put un aboard, and he went down the fo'c's'le and went to sleep. I knew it wasn't his yacht cause, I mean, she was French.

The next morning I was over Fowey Quay; and my brother said to me, "Here," he said, "The police officer come down here just now, 'n he said did I know if you put anybody on board of a yacht. Cause he said there's a man missin'."

I said, "Yeah." I said, "I put a drunk aboard a yacht," I said. "He was so full of it. "And," I said, "He went aboard of a French yacht. I said I knew it wa'n't his, but," I said, "He called me a damned Cornish idiot." And I said, "I lettun go." I said, "He's gone off to France on the yacht, I expect."

Anyhow that evenin' police officer Mr. Stamp, PC Stamp, he come down to me and he said about it. "Yeah, that's right. I said, 'I don't think that's your yacht.' 'N he said 'You don't know my yacht, and I'm not a damned Cornish idiot.' And I said, 'Oh well,' I said, 'I presumed that.' So," I said, "I let un go." I said, "He's gone over to France on the yacht, I expect."

Course he had no papers with un, no money. So his wife hadda get that off to un as quick as she could; so he could come home. I had lots of jobs like that on the ferry.

And one night some chaps came down three o'clock one mornin', 'n they wanted me to put 'em aboard their ship. So I put 'em aboard their ship. And one of 'em went up the ladder, four of 'em all together. An' the last one was goin' up; so I said, "Well, how about givin' me some money fer goin' out to bring you aboard then, payin' me for bringin' you aboard."

He said, "You wants payin'?"

I said, "Yes." So I just turned meself like that as his foot came back. He was going to kick me in the face. That was goin' to be my payin'. Yeah.

So the next mornin' I told Police Officer, PC Miles, (you remember him). "Well, I'll drop aboard that ship, Claude."

I said, "All right, sir." So I took him out aboard. I seen the chaps.

The skipper said, "What do you want?" So I told him who I was, and P.C. Miles.

I said, "I brought they four men aboard last night, and that one was the last." An' I asked if he'd give me some money for bringin' 'em aboard. I never said how much."

And he said, "Do you want payin'?"

An' I said, "Yes. His foot come back and if he'd hit me in the face," I said, "he have done a lot of damage." I said, "I want payin'."

So the Cap'n called un, an he said, "Is it right what this man said? Cause I know you didn't come aboard until very early this mornin'."

So one of them said, "Yeah, he did bring us aboard early this mornin'. But we don't know nothin' about the other incident." So the capt'n asked me how much I wanted.

I said, "As I got the police officer here, it'll be left entirely to him whether you pay me in cash or whether he take them ashore. I dunno, whatever."

"Well," he said, "If you takes them ashore, my ship won't sail, and the tide's on the way out to take her cause she's goin' to sea."

"Well," he said, "In that case, Cap'n, I'll allow you to pay the man for bringin' them aboard." And I had the pay. I think the Cap'n gave me a pound for the four of em. Well, that's more than I would have charged them. So I had a very narrow escape on that one. I think if he'd hit me with his foot he'd have caused as much damage that I wouldn't have been at work for a few weeks. Well, on the night ferry I had lots of narrow escapes.

Do you remember there was a big case in England with the train robbery? Well, I had two men and a woman, and they were on the ferry. And as I came into

Polruan Quay, a police officer - not Mr Miles, the other one - had a dog, Dino, Alsatian. And it was his own private dog, not a police dog. And Dino used to come and talk to me every evenin'. He used to come down, an I used to give un a sweet. And he came down, and this man and woman - two men and woman - they saw the dog and was worried. Woman got off the boat, went up the steps and the two men, an' I had no passengers to take to Fowey. Then I noticed the parcel. So I picked the parcel up, put it up on the side; and that evenin' when I moored up the boat, I put the parcel in the cabin. An' the followin' evenin' a woman come to me. "I live in Polruan."

I said, "Oh, do you?"

"Yes, we've got a house. My sister left her parcel. She's been shoppin' and left her parcel."

I said, "There you go, missus." So I gave it to her. When I got back to Fowey the police was there. This was a parcel of money from the train robbery. Yeah, an they want them. I think they managed to stop a car the other side of Looe. And I thought, "My gar, all that money!"

LLOYD DUNN
BORN IN 1911, SPEAKING IN 1996

In Dunn's Yard the old sailormen used to come ashore with their barrels that they'd brought from the ship and walk in to the well, which is in underneath the building which is there now, and go in there with their buckets and bail out water from the well and put it in the barrels and carry it out to the ship. It was the best water that they'd ever used in their lives. That was a hundred years ago. Well Court - that was another name of Dunn's Yard. It was the same place, yeah, I'm sure of that.

Our joy down in Polruan was to go down in Dunn's Yard and play down there with the boats when the tide went out. We turned over every pebble on the beach looking for little shrimps and little spider crabs and all that went to do with the sea, and we used to stay there till the tide come in and floated us off. We had wonderful times down in Dunn's Yard.

As I say, Dunn's Yard, that was our joy. We used to go around before the 5th of November with big grappling irons and haul down the bracken and the brambles from the cliff all the way around down in the middle of the yard and then pile it all up, get all the tar barrels that we could find. Then when it came to the 5th of November all the folk from nearby used to come around and watch us lighting the fire. Everyone was welcome - everything was free at Dunn's Yard. And then when the fire had burned down, we used to roast chestnuts and potatoes in the burning embers. And dear old Grandmother Dunn, she was there too, wearing a little bonnet on the top of her head. We loved every minute of it, couldn't go wrong. I shall never forget my childhood.

Of course then, playing with the ladder, with my brother. I hadn't learned to swim, but he had, and so had my sister. The next thing was, I fell off the ladder into the harbour. My brother began to scream; and one of my aunts - this would be Leonora Hunkin - she heard me screaming, and she ran down, didn't stop for anything, jumped right into the harbour and caught hold of me and pulled me back to the ladder and got me ashore. I was rather wet, and so was she - a wonderful woman - gift for to save life. She pulled me out and got me to shore. And since then I've been able to save one hundred and thirty persons who were in danger of drowning in our Fowey Harbour, on our cliffs, on our beaches all the way around. It all came naturally to me; all I had to do was jump in and carry on. I learned to swim, of course. But lives were very often thrown away because of alcohol; and I've never forgotten that.

Dear Mr. Jackson had a crabber down there. Now, we were dared, dared ever to go in the 'Ellen Gay'. That was his wife's maiden names. We were dared ever to go into that crabber, though she was laid up along the quay all puckered away - but we were never allowed to go into that crabber. Of course, Mr. Jackson, he was a real firebrand; and of course part of our family was the Jackson family. And then my mother's family came from sailmakers from Polruan and Polperro, the Barretts. There are Barretts still in Polperro now belonging to that family.

The joy of our life was going to school. Skipper Widlake, he was a wonderful disciplinarian. Oh my gosh, yes. He used to stand outside, and a boy would be in on the bell-rope in the school ready to ring the bell. Right on nine o'clock, "Ring!" That was his command. And the bell would start to chime. Very gifted he was. I was never taught by him, but I came into his life at the end of his life. He used to sit in there in the middle of the school before it was bombed and catch hold of the table and shake because these boys would run out of the door, run out on Polruan Hill, to get away from him.

Skipper Widlake, he had produced more Master Mariners than any port in the West Country. He was a master at it. They were all done by common arithmetic. He was a very clever man in arithmetic, navigation, anything at all.

Our joy also was to kick the football all the way down the hill right down to Polruan Quay, and two of us were detailed off to see if we could find the ball and bring it back again.

This is one of my tall ones. A dear old blacksmith from Polruan had to make a ship's anchor, and he made his anchor down in the forge down there in the back part of Polruan. And he had to carry the anchor up Fore St, where the post-office now is. In behind there was a little dwelling of some sort where they used to do their ironwork. This was a long time ago; and he carried the anchor on his back. I don't suppose it was a more than a half hundredweight. This was the story.

I used to pump the old organ for Helen Hender in both chapels. Pumping an organ, that was great fun because sometimes you would lose the rhythm of the hymn and forget when you had to pump the organ with your foot. I used to stand on one leg. I did it for Chris Blount when we were making a recording of Polruan. "Oh," he said, "No, this isn't television. You don't have to do that." I was pumping away with one hand and doing something else with the other, catching hold - there was a little brass rail that covered the organ blower. I used to catch hold of this brass rail and work one leg up and down and stand on the other one. It was most amusing really - had to go in rhythm with the hymn.

My brother went to the Grammar School. Dad couldn't afford to send me. My sister was sent to the Grammar School. Now when it came to pay for me, they couldn't afford it. So I wasn't allowed to go. "Now what are you going to do with Lloyd Dunn?"

"Well, we'll put him in the pilot boat." So I left school and went in the pilot boat and served the pilots there, all eight of them. I was always the first one to be called and the last one to get off. But it didn't matter what the weather was like. I had to go, and I had to do my job best as I could. But I always got out and back safely.

I wasn't allowed to steer. Oh, Dad always had to steer, stand up at the tiller at his back - amazing. And then eventually the time came! How old I was, I don't know, when I was allowed to steer. Oh my goodness! That was the joy of my life.

We had a lot of fun all the way, all the way around the coast. And my father used to say, "You must keep your eye out, my son!" So, of course, we went out one day for a wash-down. 'Twas a southerly-east wind, lovely breeze, and we were hammering away to the eastwards, and my father said, "You must keep your eye out." So I looked back over my port quarter.

"There's a little rubber dinghy in alongside the rocks!" Now you know what was going to happen, you only have to look. So we turned around immediately and went back. Now, how do you get alongside a little rubber dinghy that isn't manoeuvrable at all, with onshore winds; and you don't know if you can rescue them or not - a dinghy that wasn't more than afloat, with these two men rowing her right alongside the rocks all the way down past the eastern part of Pencarrow Head? I couldn't go in stern first, which is the normal practice when you come alongside a craft. I had to go in bow first. Now you're only asking for trouble when you go in bow first because your power won't stop you in time before you're on the rocks. Next thing was, I went right in there and threw our little tow rope aboard the craft.

And they made it, and they held on with their hands, and I had to reverse her out. Now you take a couple stees off the stern, which you aren't allowed to do when you're going to rescue anybody. Because that's what you have to do with the circumstances prevailing. And eventually, we turned around and got away to the sea.

So I said, "What on earth were you doing in here?"

"Oh, we've been coming here for fourteen years - it never happened before.

"But," I said, "you come down here with strong easterly winds."

"Oh no, first time we've ever done it." But we got away with it, and we got them; we got away with the craft as well. We had to take them back to Lansallos beach and landed them there.

And I said, "You'll never forget this."

"No, we probably never will."

We used to go up the river on the tide and go right up to Lerryn. Sometimes we got to Lostwithiel right on the top of the tide. Now we had to be very careful here because we weren't allowed to steer. Dad always had to steer you see, and he used to have to show us where we had to go. And then we would go up there right up to Lostwithiel, and we would turn around and come back again, sometimes stuck on the bottom. We always got away with it.

When we got to Lerryn we used to meet the old men. Mr. Bellringer, an old fashioned farmer, who used to run a little haberdashery of some sort or kind; and he was a lovely old man. These old men were wonderful old men, and they used to watch us going up and down the river.

Now, on top of this we loved to sing. This was handed down to us from generation after generation. The people in Golant used to watch us coming down there, rowing in the night - before we had a motor boat, this was. And they used to listen to the Dunns singing. We used to sing every hymn in the hymn book all the way down because we came from a very religious family. We used to go all the way down, right down past Golant, and then right down past Wiseman's Stone.

Then if ever we were allowed to go outside, to go down to Polkerris, Mother used to say, "Now you be careful of the Rags of the Gribbin!" This was a shallow patch of rock which is out off the Gribbin Head. And then we used to go down inside the Cannis Rock when the tide was high. Sometimes when the tide was low, we used to go down outside, about a mile and a half from Fowey. We loved every minute of it. All we wanted to do was to be on the sea. That is all we looked for.

And now there'd be monstrous great ships, monstrous! We'd never seen such big ships in our lives. We were only about this high, you see, but Dad was always there. He was always in charge of us - we didn't have to worry about anything because Dad was there.

And then the next thing was to see these great ships being loaded. And then Dad would take us up sometimes if he wasn't the pilot. Ships, ten thousand, eleven thousand tons, and to see these great ships going down. "Oh she's going to go ashore!" No, they always turned the corner all right, down on the straight, down past No. 1 Jetty, round the corner. Now if the ship had a right hand-propeller, you were helped in almost every corner that you came to because when you put the engine astern, it turned the ship around automatically. But it didn't always go like that because we had a lot of ships with left-handed propellers.

There on the Quay - in the early '40s we used to watch the sea coming in around at Castle Point, rising up there. And there was one of the walls there underneath the crane. The wall began to bulge out, and out went the wall, out into the harbour. My God, I don't know what it's going to do. The wall in Dunns' Yard, it fell into the harbour. Then, of course, every sea that came in around Castle Point took away hundreds of tons of the yard!

In 1959, I was asked by Mr. Toyne to go to Plymouth and bring down a great passenger liner, the 'Rosecohn', carrying nine hundred passengers. She was a monster! Now, as we came up to Plymouth, I could see what was going to happen. This was the harbour fog; our local term was called the Ornigo. Now where it comes from, morning fog or evening fog, I don't know. But that's the term that went with it. The Ornigo was coming down the river. That was a denser fog than you would get from the sea. Now of course I came up from Plymouth with this great passenger liner, and the Captain said to me - he spoke very good English -"Oh, Mr. Pilot, the ship is left-handed."

"Oh," I said, "We gotto go around right-handed." Oh, I had to think what I was going to do next. You see, you didn't have time to worry about what you had to do. You had to get on and do it. And then we came all the way right down and took on our two tugs and came in the harbour.

When you come to turn starboard to go up Pont Creek it is automatic when you put the engine astern, she will turn herself around automatically. That's no problem. It will help the ship around. This is what you want, the ship to help herself. The ship knows what she wants to do; all you have to do is help her - oh it's as simple as that. Well, we came in from there. When I put her slow astern, she wanted to go right up the main river, right up to Mixtow. No, I didn't want to go up there. Anyhow, I got over that alright, turned her around stern first; and we went right back past the ferry slip and then right back up to Mixtow.

And then we had to drop the anchors. Now to lay a ship up, you have to take special precautions. And I had to take special precautions with this great ship, and eventually we got back there and moored up on the buoys.

"Now", I said, "Captain, we have to put out the insurance wires."

"We don't have any insurance wires, Mr. Pilot. You have to moor her up with the ordinary mooring wires."

Now, this presents another problem with her because you're doing it all the wrong way. But he's the Captain, and he has to have the final say. Eventually we put out the mooring wires. The next day I had to send for the Harbourmaster. He had to go to Falmouth with his tug and bring back the mooring wires, wires as thick as my fist here, massive great things. These great wires were put out there, and she used to rise and fall there with the tide - twelve thousand tons. She was a monster. But I've never forgotten that.

Now after six months they had decided that the ship would be sold back to Zeebrugge, and there she would be cut up. Oh my goodness me! But there won't be any captain or any engineers or any crew on board. Now, you see, this is another problem you're faced with. There was never anything easy about pilotage. Well, we went up there and cast off. I shouted down to my cousins, Howard and Fletcher, on the tugs. "How much steam do you want to heave the anchor with?"

"Oh, we want two hundred pounds."

So I went to these two young Germans there as watchkeepers, "Now, how much steam do you have?"

"Oh, we can only manage one hundred and eighty". Now there's another problem, you see. You can't do what you want to do when you want to do it because there are always so many objections, and you never knew what was going to happen next.

Anyway we heaved up one anchor at a time, and eventually we set off. Now, with a left handed propeller, of course she didn't want to go down the river. I laugh about it now, but it wasn't funny at the time. And then we got down around by the ferry and down off the harbour office, and at last we were free of the harbour and got outside. So I said goodbye to the watchkeepers.

We had a great Dutch tug called the "Usthley", a massive great tug, two thousand tons. And of course there were no corners in the river for him. No, he just wanted to go straight on. And I was all the time shouting down to stop to it, and my two local tugs on the stern of the ship keeping her back, but this tug was more powerful than they were, and oh my goodness! - It wasn't funny any more, but anyhow we got outside and said goodbye to everybody. And I remember seeing the stern tug tow rope hanging right down into the water. And that was the end of the "Rosecohn", and she went off to Zeebrugge, and she was broken up.

If I go back to my father's and grandfather's day, they were sailing ship men, and Dad used to steer the ship from on the bow of the ship, you see, or sometimes he would steer the ship from on the stern of the ship. And his favourite expression was to the captain of the tug, "Take a pound, Captain Toms." That was just to take the weight off the tow rope because, you see, with a sailing ship, once you got her to go ahead, you couldn't go astern. And of course these were the problems these dear old men had to put up with.

But dear old Fred Johns, he was another, a marvellous pilot. He was gifted. What he could do with a ship was nobody's business. He did on one occasion sail a ship in from outside the river, and he sailed her in under sails and went all the way up Pont Creek and ran her up on the mud up there where she had to stay. And we were very proud of Mr. Fred Johns. He was a gifted man.

It was handed down from father to son, father to son. And my pilotage came down from my father and grandfather and my late brother. And I'm glad I had a little bit of what my father and my late brother did. We were very proud of that.

Now there were ships and ships, and there were captains and captains. I remember taking up one ship there, and we always had trouble with one thing or the other. Either the anchor wouldn't let go, or you couldn't heave the anchor up, or else you couldn't start the engine, or else if you got it to go ahead it wouldn't go astern. These were all little problems that were desperate, of course, when you're trying to do the job. But you can laugh about it now. These were wonderful men who could tackle anything - didn't matter what situation arrived, they could always deal with it.

Dear old Captain Toms - we used to hear the tug men going up in their rowing boat from Polruan up to the little tugs up off Clay Point, and then they used to get aboard, and then we used to hear them shovel coal in on the fire. And then the little tugs would go out.

It was Mother's joy and our joy too when we used to watch this great ship coming in in the night because we were being kept up. We should have been in bed you see. Well, we were rubbing our hands about this to think we were stayed up to see this great ship coming in. At last you could hear the men on the tug talking. We were in Polruan, you see, just a few hundred yards from the ship; and they were all talking to one another about what they had to do and what was next. And then you see the bow of the ship coming. Ohh! Ten thousand tons, a great monster! And then I could hear my father talking to the crew now up in the bow - he had a wonderful voice. Some of the pilots didn't have very clear voices, but his voice was as clear as could be.

I can tell you about a rescue, now, that we made with his voice on Peak Cliffs in Polruan. We went up there to look at the weather, Dad and I, and we went up and looked. "There! My! She's in trouble! Come on!" We ran all the way down peak - stood on the top of the cliffs. There was a little craft in there going from one side to the other. Wind was sou'west, but they were all seasick; and when you're seasick you want to die. They couldn't care less what was going to happen to them. And then the next thing was my father ran down. Now he gets out this big voice. "You can sail your craft into the harbour if you do what I say!"

Another man got up and said, "What do you want us to do?"

"Haul in your mainsheet, and your stay-sail sheet. You can sail in your craft down. You've no need to be wrecked here like this."

Well, of course, it thrilled us and we were delighted with it, and as this poor man got them off the deck and they hauled in the main sheet and hauled in the jib sheet; and she took herself under way and she sailed all the way back along the coast, went in around Punchy Cross and went in the harbour safe and sound. That's how you can save a ship from being wrecked with your voice, and we were blessed with that.

It was all so unnecessary, all the rescues that I've said that I've taken part in. You can only say that in every case, not ones or twos, it was quite unnecessary; it was entirely their own fault. You had to risk your life to save somebody else. They didn't know anything about it.

Schooners were still coming in for clay. They were no height out of the water. Now, there's another story that goes with that. These little schooners sometimes would come in loaded with coal for the coal wharfs. There was a coal wharf at Berril's and another one a little bit further down, and I had to learn how to put these sailing ships in on the coal wharf on the Fowey shore, and we used to have to do all of this - well it was just like having our meals and we enjoyed every minute of it. But it was quite a problem to get it all to go right.

Now, with the disappearance of the sailing ships, the little Dutch men came along who only used to navigate in the summertime. They never used to come down the channel from Holland down to Fowey in the winter because they were so small. And we used to watch these little ships coming down, and they were blowing cigarette rings over the top of the mast. This was most amusing to watch. I used to be put aboard the ship and lay down on top of the hatch coaming and watch this little ship coming in blowing smoke rings. I was thrilled with that, and I could look down into the engine room and see all the pistons going up and down and all the valves going up and down - it was most exciting to watch. This was why I was so keen with engineering.

Then the war came. And I didn't want to kill anyone. I had to go to save life as fast as I possibly could. So I was determined to save as many lives as I could by blowing up German mines.

Then, of course, I went mine-sweeping - I could save life. So I went away on the East Coast. I got up there. There were only seven thousand other sailors in the depot. Some of them knew the sharp end went first and the blunt end came afterwards. That was all they knew about the sea or ships. Well, it was most amusing. How we got away with it, we shall never know. The Lord must have been on our side.

And then the next thing was we were able to blow up these mines in shallow water because they were magnetic. Now, all the magnetic system was taken out of all our ships; so there was no attraction for the mine at all in these ships. This was what we had to do. Now, the next thing was, everyone will know what an acoustic hammer is for digging up the road. It roars away there hour after hour. When our acoustic hammer stopped, we had to stop too. Well goodness me!

Anyhow, we had a young man came and joined our ship, and I said, "What ships have you been in, my son?" Just to make conversation.

"I've never been to sea before."

I said, "Oh yes? Come on, let's go up and see the old man and send you back again." We went up to see the captain. I said, "Now look sir, this young man has never gone to sea before. I'm in the engine room, and he hasn't got a clue. He's going to be seasick." The joke was he used to watch me with my head in a bucket being seasick, but he was never seasick the whole time he was in the ship.

But the number of men that we had on the ship hadn't got a clue how the mine worked or how the ship worked. We had to teach them all everything we could. I remember going on watch one night. I said to the stoker, I said, "Go on the bridge and see what the weather's like." So he went on the bridge, and he had it all written down. "Oh," I said, "Yes, and what's the sea like?" He hadn't written down what the sea was like.

He says to me, "It's more up like this."

"You've made my night, my handsome." He hadn't a clue what he was talking about about the weather or the sea. But we were brought up to it - that's what counted.

Now, we eventually got through the war - I got promotion and went from 2nd Class Stoker to 1st Class Stoker. Then I became Petty Officer, and then I became a Chief Petty Officer. And then I was sent over to Wales just before the invasion. Now whether I should be able to survive the invasion I don't know, but I was sent over there to commission a brand new ship. She was a beauty! A 500 horse-power, super charged. This great ship would be ready to blow up mines, and we went over there and took her out and we came all the way down around the south coast and down around the Land's End, and I'm looking for the Dodman, then the Gribbin Head. "Now," he said, "This part in here, this is up in Devonshire, and he said, "We're just coming down to the Start Point."

I said, "Excuse me, sir, this is where I was born." Poor man, he didn't know what to say. "Now," I said, "We're right off Fowey now. You can't go wrong. You can get me up and show me the charts if you like, but I'll show you where Fowey Harbour is on the charts, and this is where we are now." So that put paid to that poor man.

Then we came home, and I was some thankful for that. Then on the pad there was a signal from Mr William Stone. He used to run the coal ferry. There was a big notice painted up over Stone's Coal Store. Now he decided he would buy the ferry company; so he lashes out the money. Then he came to me. He said, "Lloyd, I've decided to take you on as partner because I'm taking on Mr. Ricketts. He's a Polruan man. He'll do all the carpentry, and we want you to do the engines." The penny hadn't dropped for me, not in this time. He ran all the cash. He knew every penny that had been paid and hadn't been paid. Very clever man to handle the cash to the penny. Never owed anything. But if you owed him a penny or a ha'penny, he knew it. But I did some years there.

At the end of the war a German bomber flew down the river. Poor old Dad, it finished him. He saw this aircraft coming down Fowey River, down over Polruan, pulled a lever, and out came four bombs. Dad was looking up at this aircraft, wondering where the bombs were going to pitch. The first one pitched in that little building that was being built there, blew that one all to pieces, the next one pitched on the boys' school - blew that one all to pieces. Oh goodness me! Then the next two - the first one fell in Furze Park near to where Dad was standing. How he wasn't injured I don't know. And the last one fell into the sea.

It finished Dad. He didn't want to kill anybody, but now he was going to be killed. It didn't injure him at all. But he came home and sat in the chair, he never moved, never did anything for anybody. In three months he was dead. It was awful sad really. He only wanted to save life, and here were these damned Germans coming down Fowey River to blow our little hamlet to pieces. Oh, I shall never forgive the Germans for that.

Now, on top of that they said you gotta forgive your enemies. After the war we decided to invite a group of school children, from Germany. I don't know where they come from, but these children were brought down to Polruan and my wife said, "I'll have two." So these two children were brought down into our place, and we made them as comfortable as we possibly could. They spoke reasonable English. Some spoke perfect English, some didn't speak any English at all - that was quite a problem. But we never really wanted to forgive them for what they done to our nation. We'd lost hundreds of thousands of men in in the Navy, in the Army, in the Air Force. Men who went off to war and never survived the war. And yet now the next generation coming along - we had to turn the other cheek. There, it's in the Bible, and you do what you can for these young people and hope they will learn something from what our nation had been handed down. I shall never forget that, never.

And Mr. Fred Dunn. Now that's another story. He came home after his brother had died - that's my father's brother, Moses Dunn Jr. Mr. Fred Dunn thought he was going to have the job. But the Fowey pilots wanted to reduce their numbers from eight to seven - there wasn't employment to keep eight pilots going. So they all said no.

Now Mr. Fred was another Dunn. He would tackle anything didn't matter how rough it was. If the sea was going over the pier that never mattered to him, not a bit. He was delighted how rough it was. He had a little twenty foot open boat that he used to go out from Par all in to Polperro. If you got in the inner harbour in Polperro, you could moor up in safety. But he had to go to sea, and he used to go in to Looe. And of course, he used to look out. "Here's a ship coming down inside the Eddystone!" And he used to go.

We had a pilot cutter then, he was called the 'Sir Arthur', and we used to go off to get the ship off coming down inside the Eddystone. And sometimes he would get to the ship first, and then we would come alongside. I remember Captain Jim Salt - he went out, and Fred Dunn got in just ahead of us because he had miles between Polruan and Looe, you see - he could overcome on our speed..

The old men used to carry their food with them in pillow cases. And when we went down to get it out of the pilot-boat, Dad had put all the pasties that Mum had cooked for us in this pillow case. Well, as he got down the ladder, the stitches all broke; and all the pasties went into the harbour. Now this was the greatest insult you could ever do to a Cornishman to lose your pasty overboard.

But it was a terrible time because, on top of that, we had Richard Hughes. Hugh Evans's father was Captain of the Rose boats - the 'Primrose', the 'Guelder Rose', the 'Moss Rose', the 'Hemlock Rose' - every ship had a rose. They weren't allowed to take pilots. So, of course, these ships used to come in night and day on the mooring. And when my turn came, I came in with a two thousand tonner. I didn't know this ship had gone in and moored up with his anchor up on No 1 Jetty and with a stern line back on the buoy. So I come up around the corner to moor her up. Here's a ship moored right across the river! So now I had to find a little crack where I could put the ship through. There's only just room. Now your heart's in your mouth this time, wondering what the captain is going to say. "What have you brought me into a place like this for, pilot?"

"Well, I didn't know the ship was in here." Oh my goodness! And anyhow I got this ship up around the corner and moored her up in safety. But you had to think about the safety of the ship all the time and the crew. It was no fun, but we got away with it eventually.

Next thing was, Uncle Fred was transferred to Par. Now Par in those days, sixty or seventy years ago, wasn't a very busy port. But it gradually grew and grew and grew until Uncle Fred couldn't cope with the ships that he had there. He would have twelve ships inside and twenty outside anchored. Well, how he didn't die on the pilotage, I don't know. But he was a marvellous pilot, and he could tackle anything, didn't matter when it was or what it was. Anyhow, we used to chase him all around the seas, down to the Dodman, down to the Willies, way out to the eastward inside the Eddystone and be chasing him night and day.

When Uncle Fred was transferred to Par, he was so popular there every captain knew him. And I went aboard a ship on one occasion when I was sent down there. Fred had gone on until he collapsed, you see. And the captain said to me, "Who are you, Mr. Pilot?"

"Oh," I said, "my name is Dunn."

"Oh my God, not another one!" That really put the cat among the pigeons.

I said, "Yes sir, my father and Fred's father were brothers. We're always proud of what we tried to do to get the ships in and out."

"Well," he said, "Mr. Pilot, it's like this. I was hoping we could get away on tonight's tide. It is Wednesday today, and I could be in Liverpool on Saturday morning's tide and be home for the weekend."

"Well," I said, "I'm sorry. We can't go yet. The sea's come up over the pier. But very often the gale will break on high water, and then we can go." Well, there we were walking up and down watching the sea coming over the pier, and at last, "Come on, Captain," I said, "We can go on the ebb tide now."

When you go on the ebb tide, you're askin' for trouble. I knew I had to go, and so off we set down the river, down the dock, and we got out and turned the corner. He said, "We're all right now."

"No," I said, "Not yet, sir, we haven't started yet." We got around the piers, and then she sat on the bottom. Then these great breakers roared over the ship - she was completely under water except for the bow of the ship and the bridge. You can feel the hairs going up and down on the back of your head and your heart going like fledger of a ten ton digger. But anyhow you got to tell the captain something as to what's happening. No good saying it's nothing. I said, "Alright, captain, I see the lights moving ashore." It meant she couldn't plunge and splash herself on the bottom of the harbour because there wasn't water enough. She only just managed and slid out on to the sand there. I said, "All right, Captain, she's clear now. Oh just a minute!" Now along came another great sea. She roared over the ship.

Now I'd rigged a ladder on the port side myself all in purpose ready for getting off the ship. At last we got away clear to the sea and got out there. I said, "Well goodbye, Captain, fine passage to you."

"Goodbye, thank you very much indeed." So I ran along to get on the ladder - they'd taken the ladder away! I thought, well the only thing to do is run along the deck and and get up on the rail of the ship and catch hold the big stay that went up to keep the mast up. Then when the boat came alongside, I had to make a flying leap from the rail of the ship into the pilot boat. Eventually I got away. I've never forgotten that. I went so fast on one occasion in Par harbour that I slid down the ropes that were covered with wet china clay. You didn't stop - you went right on past the pilot boat right down into the water, then haul yourself off again.

I remember coming in with a great ship 'L'Acacia'. Captain said, "Stop the ship, Mr. Pilot!"

I said, "There's nothing going wrong with her."

He said, "No, I know. It's such a beautiful place. I want to take a photograph."

I came down from the eastward along the coast and the captain was creating. "Mr. Pilot, there's no place to go in. There are only rocks everywhere. There's no place to go in."

I said, "We'll find a crack in the rocks in a minute. I'll just go out around Punchy Cross and go right in there. Plenty of room inside." He didn't believe me.

HUGH EVANS
BORN IN 1911, SPEAKING IN 1987

My mother's name was Hunt. Her father, who had emigrated from Exeter and had married a girl in South Africa of Dutch/German extraction, had been kicked out of South Africa when the Boer War broke out in 1899, and he refused to fight on the side of the Dutch against the British. He was given forty-eight hours to leave. He came first to Bodmin, then to Polperro and after a few weeks to Polruan where he settled. Mother trained at Simeon Rowes, then worked for Singletons in Fowey, where David Evans (now Fowey River) estate agent is now.

In 1908, Father was a Master Mariner, trading in Fowey, and was skipper of the 'Briar Rose'. And during his visits to Fowey, he met my mother. And they got married and lived in Limestone Terrace, which is the little terrace just below the Polruan Post office. And it was in that little corner cottage where I was born. Then we lived one year in the Coastguard cottages, then at Moss terrace 1916-1973. They were always very much in love with each other; and when Mother finally died in 1964, Father pined and was dead within twelve months.

Father was with the Rose Line for years. Then, at the beginning of World War II, there was a job going as skipper of the steam hopper for the bucket dredger. I asked if they would be interested in Father for the job, and they said he would be perfect. You see, Father had been through World War I in the Rose Line; and he and Mother were so close, I wanted to keep him from being in another war. So he went to work for the dredger.

The original oil painting of the 'Briar Rose' by Chappell, my father had given to the Reading Room - it hasn't been seen since. It had a black funnel, with a narrow red band near the top, aft on the ship, the bridge in the middle and was three-masted.

When Tom's Yard recently filled in that little beach off East Street, there was a furore. Daphne Taylor thought there had been a public right of way and steps against the wall leading to the beach, but she was wrong. There was never even a permanent ladder to that beach. The only access was down Slades yard - private - we had to sneak down.

Out West Street there was never a public right of way down to the beach by the Coastguards out by the steps to the Castle. What used to happen was, on the autumnal and spring equinoxes, the Coastguards would grant a temporary concession to the Polruan ferrry to land there at those unusually low tides. There was, and still is, a public right of way out West Street opposite Bill Welsh's, No. 45, where that cobbled way leads down. At the bottom, instead of going into Vaughan's yard, which is private, you double back.

Now, we used to have a lot of shops, too, in Polruan that seem to have disappeared . Out at Keelson, out West Street, that was a sort of a chemist shop kept by a man named Stephens, Charlie Stephens. As in most villages in those days, we used to have nicknames of various people; and we used to call him not Charlie Stephens but Charlie Wiggie - I don't know where the Wiggie part came from. And he was a crafty old chap - he had a great big bell on his door, and it was on a string. And we used to try to open the door gently to get in without ringin' the bell. But he was a little craftier than we were. He had a little trip thing at the back of that stuck in the top of the door. And it was just impossible to get in without that bell ringin' because you had to put a little force on the door to get past the little trippin' device he had; and in doin' that, the bell would ring, and of course we'd run. But he was a dear old chap, really.

And next door to Charlie Stephens, there was a baker's shop. It wasn't a bakery but a baker's shop. That's where old Mrs. Williams used to live, Graham Williams's mum. And the bread used to come over from Fowey from Hender's of Fowey to Hender's of Polruan. And that's where we used to get our bread from, on West Street where Eileen Hunking lives now and where Mrs. Hender lived with her family; Mabel, Garfield, and Susie Hender.

. Mother lent her brother, Charles Hunt, the money to buy the bakery on Fore Street, where the bakery is now. He bought brand new ovens from Bristol, I think, and made so much money he paid her back in two years. He had a van going around with bread with Fred Phillip as driver. I don't think the premises had been a bakery before - if it was, it had been a broken down one.

And on East Street, by the steps to Hall Walk, where Mrs. Roddie Bate lives now, (behind No. 20), there was a shop there at one time. And all these have disappeared now, I suppose.

Mr. Millard, my Uncle Alan, repaired boots in the shop which was the Post Office, owned by Mr. Goldsworthy, who sold it to my uncle. It extended from the present Bakery to the Butcher's shop. At that end of the building was a door and you went in and around the back where Mrs Millard did her housekeeping.

The Post Office moved to a shop fronted building opposite the Co-op place. Two girls I remember working there were Alma Lewis and Muriel Wright.

The Crapps used to live where the butcher is now. Holton made it into a butcher's shop. Hedley Cossentine was in where the Co-op was later - a carpenter, undertaker, sold wallpaper. I remember wood work going on in the shed at the Palmers up Fore Street and coffins being made.

Polruan was never what you'd call affluent. The clay trade in those days was not that brilliant - not much work. Besides that, it was mainly local fishermen - we never starved because there was always fish. There was work up the jetties - well, you went up the jetties, signed on twice a day, fifty men maybe, first thing in the morning. If your face suited, you got the job. It wasn't first come, first get the job. One man might go up twenty times and get work once; another might get work almost every time. Then the Dock Labour Board scheme came in between the wars. All registered as dockers and got paid even if there was no work. Before that, it had been a real scramble.

There was a windmill at the top, just outside the village, which had four metal legs, maybe six by six, like an electricity pylon going up, tapering criss-cross to a platform at the top. There was a ladder going up the outside. I climbed to the top platform, ninety-two feet up. The machinery for the windmill was placed on this platform and four blades, and the shaft came down the centre to work the generator underneath. The blades were fixed not feathered so not all that successful. The platform was fixed to face southwest; so that it didn't rotate with the wind and so was a failure. The windmill didn't light everyone's houses at all. It did supply a certain amount of electricity but was very erratic - had storage batteries; but the output was more than the input.

What kept the village going was the Lister generator in Tom's Yard which was switched on just before dusk till 11:00 pm, direct current. Joe Connor, my uncle, ran it. Dr. Jay had all the poles put up around the village, brought electricians from Plymouth. I was an apprentice for a while working with them. Polruan was the second village in the county on electric, and the first village was Mevagissey.

How self sufficient was Polruan? People needed to go outside the village for surprisingly little. The work was mainly clay, coal, wood, fishing. If a man was not a

Docker, then he was doing casual work unloading coal at Stones on the Wharf, or stone up Pont Pill - stone from Plymouth and Port Haustock near the Lizard. The 'Shamrock', 'JNR', 'PHE', 'Mayblossom', 'The Sirdar' came with stone. The 'W.E. Gladstone', Capt Hunkin of Polruan, father of Fletcher and 'Siah came often. 'Siah Hunkin was a fisherman, went to live in Mevagissey.

The thing that was different then about Polruan, compared with today, was that there were very few visitors. People just hadn't heard of Polruan then. Today most people know where it is. There were hardly any guesthouses then; I can't remember any.

I'd like to tell you a little about my school days. I went to the Council School up here, to start with, which is now a car park, Town Trust car park. There was a school there. Unfortunately, it was bombed in the war. But I went there till I was about eleven, I think, and I passed my exams to go to Fowey Grammar School. But I would say that my best school days were spent in Polruan School.

And as far as goin' to the loo was concerned, there was no flush toilets as you see today, indoors. We had to go out across the yard, to start with. They used to be called "Bucket and Chuck it". But after a while, of course, they put flush toilets in. Very primitive that was, really. But as time progressed, things got better. And now they've, of course, progressed; and things, as I see now, are first class, as they should be. School days were very nice.

We had, to start with, a headmaster called Widlake - we used to call him Skipper Widlake. And he was a strict disciplinarian. And if you said anything or done anything out of turn, you would suddenly hear a command, "Walk to the desk." And as soon as you heard that, you knew that you were in for something, two of the best, at least. I never had to bend over and get it on my bottom at all, but he used to give me two of the best on occasion. And I think I deserved it.

At the Boys' School Standards I, II, and III were in a small room; Standards IV, V, and VI were in the main hall. The bell tower was in the centre of the building; so the bell rope hung down next to the wall in the main hall. Now Skipper Widlake was very stern and one for the cane; he kept it always beside him. He would say, "Evans, come to the desk!" And you would have to go up to the desk and hold your hand out for a stroke of the cane. If you tried to let your hand drop slanting down to deflect the force, he'd rap your hand underneath saying, "Up, up" to get it in position to rap square.

Percy Hanson was one who often got the cane for no reason. One day Mr. Widlake said, "Hanson, come to the desk".

And Percy said "No". As Mr. Widlake came over, we were all watching, and Percy climbed up the bell-rope right to the rafters where he stayed and refused to come down. You can imagine, there was no chance of order in class then. Finally Mr. Widlake promised not to cane him if he came down, and he did. Well, Mr. Widlake couldn't cane him then, not with all of us having heard him promise. I don't think he ever caned Percy again. Mr. Widlake ruled through fear with the cane. Mr. Roberts was all for sport. If he'd been head, we would probably have all been great athletes but imbeciles. Mr. Tipping didn't cane but was a real disciplinarian, won the boys' respect.

Anyway Skipper Widlake - he was getting on at the time - decided to retire. And just after he retired, they brought in another temporary headmaster by the name of Roberts. He was a very popular headmaster simply because he was more interested in games than he was in teaching. And we spent, I think, more time up on the hill kickin' a football around than we did in the classroom. Well, during the time that Roberts was here, the Educational Authority decided to appoint a permanent headmaster. And it happened to be a man named Tipping, Samuel Lawler Tipping, whose home, if I remember rightly, was in Everton, Liverpool.

And when the news got around that Mr. Roberts wasn't going to be the permanent headmaster, we boys decided we'd go on strike, which we did. And we were out for a considerable time. And during the strike we used to wander around - you know what boys are like - not up to any serious mischief but, you know, making a bloomin' nuisance of ourselves. Unfortunately we were backed by our parents and we stayed away for a long, long time.

Anyhow, there was a song at that time, and I remember it quite well, and I'll just sing it a moment. It goes like this;

Vote, vote, vote for Mr. Roberts!

Chuck old Tipping down the street.

If I had a treacle tin,

I would smash his head right in,

And he wouldn't see daylight any more.

Well that song we used to sing all around the village to the delight of some of the older ones, I suppose.

But eventually, we had to go back to school, and Mr. Tipping came down. Mr. Roberts went away. For a while we thought Mr. Tipping was a real ogre. He was a strict disciplinarian. We didn't like him at all. But eventually we came to realize that he was not only a strict disciplinarian, he was a darn good schoolmaster too. And I think many a boy who went to that school have been grateful in the years that followed that Mr. Tipping was their headmaster because he was a splendid headmaster.

And I suppose, really in those days, he had a lot to put up with. There was no such thing then, you know, as school meals. During our lunchtime we used to dash home, grab what was on the table, scoff it down, and dash back again and get on with the business of learning.

We used to get up to all sorts of tricks, you know. One of the things we used to do in our spare time - we never used to go around vandalizing like some of the youngsters do nowadays. We wouldn't smash things up. We used to play little pranks, and I'll give you an instance. We used to stuff newspapers up a metal drain pipe, light with a match; and the fire roared up the drainpipe.

Very often we used to raid Mother's sewing box and take a reel of cotton thread out. And we used to get a pin or a drawing pin and a nail, and we used to make fast the drawing pin at the end of the cotton. And about six inches in, we'd attach the nail. Then we'd go around to, perhaps a little cottage in the streets somewhere, where we would stick the drawin' pin into the putty of the framework and then unreel the cotton, go around the corner, and start pullin' the cotton, with the result that the nail would tap the window. When we could hear the door about to open, we'd stop. The owner of the cottage would just come out and have a look around, couldn't see anybody or anything, go back, and shut the door again. We gave the owner perhaps a couple of minutes to settle down; then we'd start tappin' again, you know. Eventually he used to get the idea that somethin' wasn't right; so instead of just coming to the door, he would just come outside and start investigating. When he started that, we were off. Little things like that. And it was, it was great fun. As I say, we put a nail in; we didn't put a great big nut or anything like that, that would smash the window. Little things like that.

Another thing we used to do, if we saw two doors together, two cottages - I know of two cottages out in West Street - I remember as a boy we'd go along with a bit of rope. And we'd tie the two knobs together and knock at the door. And we went down in under Grey House under the wall to see what would happen. And sure enough the two owners would come out, and they'd try to open the door - one was pullin' against the other. We thought that was great fun. Naughty, I suppose, but there you are. Little things like that.

And another thing, on the quay, which is now a car park again, that used to be an open space. We youngsters used to go down there and play on the quay. And one of the games was what we called Toss-Toss. It meant that we could play with anything from, say, six boys on each team. And one boy would stand up against the wall, and the other five boys would - the first one would put his head into the stomach of the leanin' post, as we callun, then the other boys would line up underneath him bending down. And the other team of six would - each one would jump in across the top of them, try to get in as far as they could. And some of the boys could jump right into the leaning post. That's why we had a leaning post cuz if he wasn't there, they'd probably hit their head against the wall. And the idea was that if we were to get all our six members on top of these other ones, they'd try to keep us up for ten seconds. If they collapsed, they had to stay there again; and we had another jump. But if they held us up, then it was their turn to come in; and they'd jump on us. The idea being that if you could get two or three boys, one on top of the other, onto one boy who was leanin' down on the quay, he's gonna collapse under the strain of three on top of him, you know. It meant that you had to be good jumpers to ever win the game. Just little things like that used to amuse us.

And another thing we weren't allowed to do - the linney that is on the quay now where the youngsters go in and play with their radiograms and all that - we as boys weren't allowed in there because that was where the fishermen of Polruan and the old men used to go in and have a yarn. And I've been in there before or walkin' in when the old men were havin' a little yarn, and I'd go in and try to listen to some of it. And all of a sudden they'd say, "Hello, me sonny, what's your name?"

"Oh," I'd say, "I'm Hughie Evans."

"Oh yes, and what 'e doin here then?"

"I just comin' in and have a look around."

"You know what? You come in here to listen to our conversation, I'm sure. Now I think you better run away now. Now you clear off. Off you go, clear off. Men are talkin'." And of course you had to clear off. Because they'd get 'e. And that's one of the things that happened.

And then, of course, every 1st of May used to be Tin Kettle Day. But before the 1st of May, all the youngsters used to collect all the tins they could find and rope em up. And on the 1st of May they used to start at the top of the hill and drag it right down through the hill, right down through the main street, out to West Street, East Street, all around and again. Well, of course, no question that we incurred the wrath of the older people. And they used to complain, and one or two complained to the local policeman - in my time Holman, PC Holman. A kindly police officer he was, really; but he was only doin' his duty and tryin' to stop us from not only makin' a noise, but tearin' up the streets. I mean, it wasn't tarmac in those days. They were reasonably well built; but with tin cans and tin kettles goin down the road, it was tearin' it to pieces, you see. Well, we were on the quay one day, and along came PC Holman, and he started cuttin' all the tins off or cuttin' the rope that held the tins together, thinkin', of course, that would do the trick. Course, one bright boy thought, well, wire was better 'n rope. So we wired them all up then and started afresh. And the next thing, as we were goin' down the hill, there was PC Holman comin' down chasin' us. As we were youngsters, a little bit faster than he was, we were gaining; but as we went down the hill, we all scattered. And PC Holman had to get wire cutters or pliers 'n all that, and he had one hell of a job to get rid of this lot. Anyhow, he eventually did. And, of course, a few years later the Tin Kettle Day disappeared amongst other things.

But I did like my schooldays. And I was privileged to be asked to attend a meetin' which was convened by the Reverend May who was here in my younger days. And Mr. Granville Ram, Reverend May, and Walter Brennan, "Matlo", as we knew him, myself, and Molly South, Miss South. We started the original Polruan Youth Club. Sir Granville Ram was the president, the Reverend May, at that time, was the Chairman, I was the secretary, and Molly South was the treasurer. We had a very successful youth club for three or four years, I think. It was great fun, thoroughly enjoyed it.

When we first started, we had the Church hall - it's now part of a house - and we used to have table tennis. The County Organizer at that time was a man named West, a Mr. West. I got him up from Truro, and he gave us several lectures on different things. We had table tennis, we had football, all sorts of indoor games. And

Mrs. Williams, Muriel Williams, Graham's wife, and my wife were tea hostesses. They baked things. At that time I'd gone through my bronze and gold medals, and I started to teach dancing in the end. But mainly it was table tennis, all sorts of indoor games, and we had a little dancing session at the end and a good old nosh up at the end of the evening. My wife was particularly keen and very good at making doughnuts, and they used to go like anything. And Muriel was very good at helping. A number of people would come up as well. "Matlo" - Walter Brennan and Gordon Elliot used to be here. Lots of people helped, oh yes, lots of people, male and female. We used to make our own fun and it was great fun, oh yeah.

It was very, very good. And of course we got our own boat, bought our own rowing boat - had it built and did rowing as well. All sorts of rowing.

After three years I was getting to the tender age of like twenty-nine or thirty. Time I was getting too old for that sort of thing, and I resigned. And I think - I'm not quite certain but I think - Mrs. Vincent took over. It went on for quite a while. I was then going to sea and away from Fowey quite a while. But when I came back I found out it had been disbanded for some reason or other, I dunno quite why. But during my time there we all enjoyed ourselves.

MAVIS TOMLIN COCKS
BORN IN 1916, SPEAKING IN 1989 AND 1997

I can remember my father, Reginald Tomlin, taking me to the Corner to see a dancing bear and can also remember an organ grinder coming to Polruan with a little monkey on a chain, who would take off his little red cap to collect money. These travellers went from village to village and that was how they made a living, usually part of a Travelling Fair.

There was another man called "Rocky Beef" who travelled around with a most weird contraption and he earned his living sharpening knives, scissors and shears. He also mended umbrellas and pots and pans. His charge would be just a few pence. During the summer Rocky Beef would be seen at most fairs, and then he would be selling shells of cooked limpets and winkles. His "pitch" in Polruan would be the Quay.

Another man would travel around buying rabbit skins, and these he would stuff into big Hessian bags. We had a rabbit meal or two every week, and most families did. We always hoped the skins would be collected fairly regularly or else

122

they would begin to smell a bit. The rabbits to be sold would be strung along a long pole and carried on the shoulder. Rabbits made cheap, tasty and nourishing meals, and Polruan people certainly liked them.

When there was a good catch of pilchards, one of the men would stand at the Corner and shout, "Pilchards, pilchards, pilchards!"; and the women would run with bowls and have quite a lot for about sixpence. My mother, along with all the other women, would clean the fish and cut off the heads and then salt them in big earthenware jars to make nice tasty meals all the winter. Served with boiled potatoes and dabbed with butter, it was really very nourishing and yet cost very little. Cornelius Pill used to sell three or four spider crabs, which we called "skellies",for about threepence - another nice meal.

I can remember on Saturday mornings the farm people and gardeners pulling down the river in their boats from Lerryn and Golant and selling on the quay their eggs, butter, cream, fruit, vegetables, flowers, rabbits, and so on, and Polruan people waiting anxiously for them to arrive. Some of these sellers were called Mutton, Bellringer, and Dingle. The Dingle family came by road in their horse and cart. The produce was always so fresh and reasonable.

My father was a Docker, and he and his mates really worked the cargo boats with shovels, and hard work it was, too. My brothers and myself were quite used to seeing our Dad come home like a snowman, covered in clay from top to toe one week. And then the next week he would become a black man, because then he would be covered all over with coal dust.

And then the more serious memories of funerals. These were far different to the practice of today. Now we have the motor hearse along with the attending cars. Today the coffin is put in a Chapel of Rest or the local Church or Chapel. I remember the dead person being kept in his or her home with family life being carried on as usual. The coffin was carried all the way out to Lanteglos by bearers. There would be about four sets of bearers and each set ready to take its turn till Lanteglos was reached. The mourners and friends walked behind the coffin and carried the flowers. Not the wreaths and ornate arrangements of today but usually bunches of flowers tied with a bow of ribbon. Families wore deep mourning and black armbands and ties were worn for quite a while. When the horse-drawn hearse came into use, the mourners and friends still walked.

In fact everyone walked almost everywhere - quite usual for some to reach Polperro or even on to Looe. After Church or Chapel on Sundays, all the family would enjoy a walk up around the hill or out the road. I myself, when teaching at Whitecross, walked there and back in all weathers and found it to be no hardship.

The land where the Council Houses quite near to Polruan School now stand, was a big field; and this was divided up into sections to form Polruan Allotments. Polruan men applied for a section and grew the family vegetables there. My father was one of these, and I can remember him hauling seaweed and bags of soot and lime to use in the growing of the veg.

Christmas Eve was wonderful, when the village men went through Fowey, Bodinnick, and out around to all the farms and big houses and sang carols, finishing in the early hours of Christmas morning at the Corner, by Shipshape, to sing the carols to Polruan people. That was when I first heard our own favourite "Rolling Downwards" and also "Hail Smiling Morn". Lovely carols, and thinking of them singing, my father and Norman and Nat Hunking, Uncle Rupert Tomlin, and so many, many others become very clear in my thoughts and memory.

I mustn't forget the pure magic of Christmas then. For weeks beforehand the house would have the tantalizing smells of nutmeg, cinnamon, ginger, saffron etc. as the mincemeat, cakes, pies, and stuffing were all homemade. Ginger wine too was carefully made and bottled and how we children would cough and splutter when given little sips of it! We helped with the stoning of raisins, etc. eating some of these delights on the quiet - and in fact we loved to sip and sample everything. That was part of the magic of Christmas. A wonderful time!

Thinking back, I'm sure the remarks of Kitty Williams were most apt. None of us were all that well off, yet we all seemed to be happy and contented and all ready to share. All mothers then made lovely, tasty, nourishing meals for a few pence.

I was born in 1916; so my mother used wash-day methods of 1900 onwards. What a business wash-day was when I was a child! No washing machines or spinners - no electric irons or driers - no rotary driers either! Monday was wash-day and it took all day. The wash-house was a necessity and in the wash-house was the "copper" under which a fire was lit to heat up the water. The whites were boiled in the copper. The coloured kept separate. Heavy clothes such as men's working trousers were scrubbed separately and thinking of men working at the jetties in coal one week and perhaps clay another week and of course fishermen with their heavy-duty clothes, the garments were quite literally scrubbed.

A "dolly tub" was on hand filled with clean water in which a Reckitt's blue cube had been put. The time was essential. Left in too long and the water was too blue. This tub was kept for the clean rinsed white articles to be put into. The Reckitts cube added that bit of blue for a good finish.

There was also a pan with starch in it ready to receive collars, table-cloths etc. The starch was necessary to give the collars etc the perfect finish. Everything was done to get satisfaction.

When everything was washed and rinsed there was the business of the wringer - two rubber rollers and a handle which squeezed the water out of the washing. Then the drying. Two big poles and a long line with a pulley to manipulate it. Just imagine the heavy flannelette sheets being pegged out using the old-fashioned wooden Gypsy pegs! I can well remember the Gypsies bringing these around for people to buy. When the weather was bright and breezy it was a bonus for the women. Good drying weather. But what a nightmare when it was misty or rain. Then lines were hung across kitchens and back rooms to peg the washing on. Smaller items were placed on a clothes-horse in front of the coal fire to dry. (I've still got one of these. It must be sixty-five years old!)

And what about the ironing? No electric steam ones then. We had a box iron which opened for the hot coals to be put in. The little irons were got hot in a glowing fire and woe betide the poor ironer if a smut or two got on the whites! I've heard my mother say many a time that it was "a fair old business" and really it took a hard day's work to accomplish.

One memory I have is this. Our mid-day meal on wash-day was always Bubble and Squeak, and I loved it. This was the remains of Sunday lunch all mashed up together - swede, cabbage, potato - and fried till it was crisp and brown. There might be an egg or cold meat with it, and it was one of the few days when we were allowed to have HP sauce. This was a rare treat for us.

I can remember a house near the Quay. There were really big heavy rollers, and people could take their piles of dry clothes to this place and for a few pence, items such as towels, sheets, vests etc. could be pressed. This saved a lot of ironing done at home. I seem to remember it took two people to work these rollers, and I think the charge was a few pence a "flasket", the latter being an oval shaped straw plaited basket. Today it would be made of plastic.

When I think back on the back-breaking wash days of my mother's time and compare them with the ease of modern days, I can almost hear my mother saying, "They don't know they're living." And that's quite true, isn't it?

Roddie and Audrey Simmons Bate
BORN IN 1922 AND 1925, SPEAKING IN 1996

(Audrey) My father's father must have come from Gloucester on a boat or something cuz there were no other Simmons like that name there. And he died quite young. He went up on a boat one morning and dropped dead on the deck of a schooner and left Grannie with seven boys to bring up. She had to go out to work. She used to go out washing clothes, spend all day in people's places, out in the wash-house washin' clothes, cleaning, doin' anything. Had to. You didn't have any money keeping children in those days.

My mother came from Falmouth, and her mother had four children includin' herself. And she died, and then my grandfather down at Falmouth married again and had five more children. And then he had a third wife, and she died, and the child died. Not long after he died and left these nine children.

Now a lady called Fox, who were big Quaker people down at Falmouth, put my mother in a home, kind of a home for trainin' girls to go into service. She put her out there. The others were all split up. The second family of five all got split up and went with aunties and grannies and uncles and whatever, and that was that. That was what had to be done. There wasn't nobody else to look after them.

Reverend Parker, that came to Polruan all those years ago, whose wife was buried outside the harbour. I was the first baby to be christened in Polruan by him. And he got talking to my mother, and he said, "Well I'm darned," he said, "I took the funeral for that mother," he said, "And I wondered what happened to those children." And my mother was one of the children he was talking about.. Wasn't that funny he should meet up with her after all those years?

Bessie Bate's husband was a Port Isaac man. That's where he come from. They had a sailing ship, his father. His father was called William Hicks Bate, and he's buried at Soulin Daniel, that's Wadebridge. In the '14 war they falled out aboard the ship. And he took off and joined the Royal Navy and never went back no more.

He met up with Roddie's mother, and she was working for Reverend Walke in St. Hilary. When Reverend Walke moved from Polruan, Bessie went down there and worked in the house.

They was out of a Sunday or somethin', and they must have met up. I think the Reverend down there said she met up with this young sailor or something and then got married. We have got a photograph of her. She was pretty when she was young; she was a nice lookin' woman like you know. And, of course, they were married in about 1914, I think.

After that he got married and came here. And then, of course, he worked on the docks. But when there wasn't a lot of work in the summer, he would go on the sailing boats, you know, fer people with money, and he'd go as the crew like. They would go on yachts for peanuts, more or less. They'd buy him a suit and a hat and what-e-call, all the gear for yachting. But they'd get about £3 a month, that's all they'd get.

(Roddie) There were two black steam barges, the larger one the 'Thames', the smaller, the 'Goliath'. They were used for bunkering the ships, owned by Stephens in Fowey. Each could take seventy ton of coal in turn from Stephens to the ships. The steam coal was kept where the Sailing Loft is between Gallants and Berrill's (in Fowey). Rod Dow and my father used to work at that.

We lived down there East Street. I was born in 1922 at the end of East Street. They two sets of steps, i'n't they, the Moss Terrace steps and the other. Well, we lived in that house between, right on the road, where the Miss Herberts lived. And Joyce Ward lived in the next one. There were six of us. There was Arthur, William, Jimmy, me, and Bernard. Pat wasn't born then.

At school you'd raise your hand to leave school at 11:40 to carry father's dinner in basket. We had to be careful not to upset the gravy. There was a thermos, a metal can with cup attached to top. It was put on stove to keep warm, tea. We took ferry, walked through Fowey to the docks. Most men went to work there by boat, three in a boat, the middle one with pair of paddles, one in stern, one in bow with one paddle each.

The Slades had a big boatyard here in Polruan, doin' repairs to ships and one thing and another. And we used to go down there and watch them makin' ships' masts, chipping away with the spar and pole - you know, tree - and they were marking in different sections, and then use an adze to chop around back to front, and trimming un off all the way around. And they would do that with their adze. They never had electric planes or anything. They had big heavy wood planes.

And they would bring timber in from up the river - they would cut timber - big trees - and bring un down by boat. Now see, a lot of people say when you said that to 'em would say, "How did they get they big trees in boats?" They never did. They used to get um with the tides. They would tie ropes onto the tree; and when the tide rose, they would pick up the ends of ropes and tie un across the boat up tight. When the tree bumped up against the bottom, then they knew they gottun, and then they'd row un home. But the log was on the outside; it wasn' in the boat. The men in Slade's Yard, where Back Beach, we called un, where Toms have filled in, they would tie they poles against the quay and leave un - oh I dunno - five, six weeks or longer to seize them in the water. That's how timber in they days was seized in the water.

And you'd go up to Devonport Dockyard, and you wanted a pole for a mast, like eighty feet, they had one there. But it was always in the river. You'd pick out the one you want and say the size, and then shipped down here by boat to do the job.

See the flagstaff on the hill where the Coastguards were. The Coastguards were up there then, and they would put up all the flags daytime. And night-time they would have lights on the poles. And I was thinkin' in here the other day, they had one pole with a glass ball on the top like that. And do you know what that was for? To tell exactly how many hours in the day the sun shined. They had this ball up there with a metal frame at the back like a banana skin (curved around the ball). But pushed in behind every day at a certain time was a piece of paper, blue. And they would push that in around and leave un there all day. And as the sun shined on that ball, 'e would burn a hole along the card. If the sun wa'n't out 'e wouldn't burn would 'e? It would go on and on and you'd meet up again. They used to change that one every day and where you marked the days and all that and the time he was put in and took out. And they was sent out - I don't know where they used to send un. But people wouldn't think of that now, you see..it was a pole, a square one, usually about five by five. Now, it was up out of the way of the kids; so that the coastguards could pull the card out and put'n back. It was as simple as that.

When I was a child, Brazen Island only went so far as where the big winch was. All the rest was bare. There was a couple of little beaches. And we could on the half tide, we could walk right around to Carne Beach. You could walk along there..

But Toms's, where Toms's slipway is, that was built and washed away when I was a kid. There was a ship's store and what we call a dry dock, there, and they used to put baulks of timber across the front. And they used to take in four-masted schooners there and put the baulks down. And she stopped there all night. It would flood out when the tide came in, but it was protected by the baulks in the back. But when we was kids all that washed away.

There was great big sawpits dug in the ground. I believe there was two , and one was right opposite where that little arch is in the bottom, used to be full up with water. Big sawpit, and they used to put big trees there, one man down the pit with a pit saw pulling down and the other pulling up. And they sawed big trees back through like that with a great big pit saw like a cross-cut saw, but a bigger one, a longer one. There was one over to Bodinnick boatyard years ago - a long one that was what they called a pit saw. A bloke would be down under. He would pull un down and the other pull un back.

Slades had a yard in Polruan then and Bodinnick, Butsons used to build in there, see. There was yards everywhere. Whitford's yard in the Yacht Club - there was a shipwright's yard there, see. Dunn's yard was being used. Then Bunts were building. They had where you had, now Polmarine. Albert Stephens was where Dinghy Club was. His father had it, P.H. Stephens - they called him "Mottle" Stephens. He used to build some boats. He lived there, or he worked from there - he had right behind Captain Joe Shea. They had a boatyard see, but they would build smaller boats, fishing boats like, a smaller type fishing boat - they had to be sailing boats in they days.

There was paths different places, like where Raymond Langmaid is, up they steps, there was a path went right through into Back Lane. Well then, when someone else bought that it, they blocked it off. "You boys not allowed!" And there was a path down the back of Waterfront, down on they rocks come out by that shed. And where they went down past Terry Curtis's and down to Jimmy Salt, there was a path right down through there to get down to the rocks. But gradually it was shut off like. There were heaps of paths. Fowey was exactly the same. They was paths led from the road to the beach. This side, in Polruan, there was one down by Russell Tomlin's, down over the steps on to Back Beach. But their argument was, when John Willie took over, it was only there for if you was trapped on the beach when the tide come in. You could go up that way, but you couldn't go down that way. Where Mary Mitchell lives, down it come out where the cafe, there was one down through there. And then they were gradually closed off like, see.

When we dug out and put Dorothy's garage in through the garden. The reason why they couldn't do nothin' about it was it was on Mrs Webb's deeds that she sold it. But in they days it was cheaper to say, "You give me the £15 in the hand. Then we won't go to lawyers, and we won't bother. That's your bit of ground." And that's how they used to do it. It was never took off their deeds.

That's why you find a lot of people in Polruan have a bit of garden belonging to next door, and they don't have any garden. Up in Moss Terrace you've got a lot of houses have gardens, some haven't. They've got a double bit. Well, the people who lived in the house decided they didn't want their garden, and the man next door was a good gardener, and he could do with that bit. So he give 'em perhaps £50 or whatever, and he'd have their garden, and they don't have any. They wouldn't go nowhere and worry to pay a lawyer to do it. They would say, "How much do you want for it?"

"So and so."

"It's yours." The man in the first house at the top of the steps of Moss Terrace has two pieces of garden down over the wall. Now then, Hughie Evans didn't have any; and Pat lives next door - he doesn't have any. But the person next door got, perhaps, a couple of bits you see. That's what happened. They parted with their gardens for a bit of money.

Well, there was an old man, and he used to come to Polruan. And he used to buy people's death policies years ago, when I was a child. An old man called Mr Keast used to come on a Monday, and he was one of these men that went around selling bits and pieces. And if somebody wanted some money or if somebody died and they didn' have money for the funeral, he would buy it. Or if they was in need of money, not necessarily a funeral, he would buy their policy if they had a death policy or something. And then when he used to came visiting the village, he used to say, "Is so in so still alive?" Or, "Is what ee call still alive." And if they had died he would say, "Oh, I must go! I must put in that there policy and claim the money." It was what they called a paid up policy, and he would buy one for some money.

Collister did Sunday dinners; Christmas dinners etc. in his oven twenty years. Obvious - had to keep coal fire going anyway. 'Singing Kettle' had cloam ovens. Bill Rawson's wife took on breadmaking with her father, Parsons, delivering by hand in big square baskets. Parsons had his run. I delivered bread for Lawry Hunt's brother. My brother worked in the bake-house and delivered. Three men (two men and a boy) used to deliver Saturday mornings in Polruan and Fowey. Mr. Hunt's brother was a perfectionist as a cook - bread, cakes - masterpiece at it - won hundreds of prizes for it.

Mr. Hunt used to deliver bread and pies, etc. from the Bakery here in Polruan over to Fowey. Mr Northey took pies and pasties and cakes Saturday afternoon to Fowey, sold in baskets. Mr Hender started bringing bread over to Miss Parson's at the beginning of the War. Saffron cakes, bread in baskets. He'd row from Albert Quay in all weathers. Old Mr Parsons had died. Used to go down on Quay in white trousers and tee-shirts.

Lorries would stop up Lady Ram's with lamp oil and petrol. They wouldn't come down the street. Old Mr Crapp would bring it down in cart and pony. Mrs Toms up in store above Ferry Store would deliver by hand - couple gallons. First lorries to go down Polruan Hill were Brook Bond tea lorries - "Trojans". Solid tyres, chain driven. Delivered tea and coffee. They tarmaced Fore St. Hill when I was in infant school.

Run up Mrs Cossentine's, where Spar is, to get sample rolls of wallpaper for Mother to choose from. You'd take a bundle of half a dozen home to try, bring them back and take more until you found what you wanted. She wouldn't pay over sixpence a roll. You could also buy there six pennyworth of putty, wrapped up in waxy paper, to do up the windows. Could buy so many screws, or paint and linseed oil. Mr Cossentine had an undertaking business out back.

Years ago you never could buy paint like now. It came in powder. You had to mix your own with water and linseed oil. Tom's Yard would have big barrels of linseed oil and rows of tins of different colours of powder, red ochre, green, blue.

Boats all used to be black. That was cheap. You went up to the gas works and bought a bucket of tar for a shilling. That was used to paint the boat and also the lower walls of cottages - it kept the green off. the upper parts of cottages were whitewashed.

There was lots of men used to come to the village selling things before the war. They used to come in here cuttin' your hair, and mother had to pay the insurance to un. What the hell was he called? He worked in the court here. Casey Court they used to call it.. He used to come Saturday mornings. They sold their insurance policy because they couldn't afford to run it. And sometimes they couldn't afford to keep it going and paying it up. And sometimes they needed a bit of money for somethin'. It all depended on the circumstances.

Unknown to people today, if a father was out of work and his sons were out of work, they could only draw the dole for one. The boys wouldn't get none. Because you were out of work, you couldn't go over and sign up - that wasn't so. You couldn't do that. You had to be in work, or you got nothing at all. Father had to keep you, and hardly keep you. It was only pittance anyway - it was only about ten shillings or something like that. It was nothin'.

But what they used to do, and as I said before, you go up on the wall, that wall that runs along the outside by the car park, and you look down over, and you look down there, as I do lots of times. And people say, "Don't it look beautiful?" And then they start. "Who lived there?" and "Who lived here?"

And I say, "You see all they gardens down there. Everyone got a bit of garden. Now they had no money, but they would do all their gardens up. But 'e was always tilled with vegetables. You never see gardens with flowers. They wasn't interested in that. They wanted something to eat - cabbages, turnips, carrots and all that. And up the top was always left about eight or nine feet for chickens. Well, everything that would come out of the garden or off the table, all that was boiled up and give to the chickens. Well, they would have half a dozen eggs a week out of they.

And we used to use isinglass. You could go to the chemist and buy isinglass, which was a pickle. You could pickle the eggs in a bucket, and they'd last twelve months. We used to do that. You'd stir them up in the water; and every time you had eggs, you dropped 'em in and leave them twelve months in that bucket. Then you could fry 'em or boil them. You could get isinglass like a treacle tin at the chemist. You mixed it up. It had its instructions on the tin. I don't think they sell it now. We used to pickle all sorts when we were first married.

We ate rabbits till we looked like 'em. Oh God, I can't face another rabbit cuz you had to skin em, you know, and everything. I used to catch rabbits in the fields there just above the houses just after the war and before. Roddie was a tradesman. He only had about £4 a week, that's all we had, rent, rates, smoke, went to pictures. Mind you, time we got to Thursday, I didn't have any money, and had to have half a crown from Mother to tide me over till the next day. They don't know them livin' these days.

Years ago the meat and that come Saturday. They would sell it off. They never had freezers to freeze it. And my mother would go in and buy a bullock's heart for a shilling. Well now, that is five pence now.

Oilskins, they were oilskins. They would hang them up with a broom handle or brush and oil them all over black tar, and they stand up and look at ee - they'd be hard as a bullet. They used to wear leather boots, what they call sea boots, but they was leather. And the bottoms had metal studs in em, you know, made sparks.

Cargo ships came to quay to unload. More or less flat bottomed, just leaned against quay. They put out a heavy beam to one side to balance. Father got sixpence a ton unloading coal in baskets, plus half pint of beer a day. There was two or three days work in some of them (110 ton some were). They put a running plank on to boom of vessel six feet off from quay. The boom was protected by bags thrown over. Then there was a trestle with scales on quay and large platform each side, weights in centre. The hold was uncovered - hatch covers were planks with two to four foot handles and covered in tarpaulins for waterproof. Two men were down hole digging out coal, two men on a winch to get coal up. Men had pads on shoulders and flour bag hoods - one corner put into other and tied around waist to keep off the dust.

Sand was brought from Golant Bar about 1930. The Bunny brothers lived at Cliff opposite Golant. They had a big rowing boat, as big as Slim's red one and double skinned inside with planks, to carry sand. Two or three ton of wet sand. they would row down to Golant Bar, wait for tide to go out, load barge, float off, and come down to Polruan, unload at the quay, and row back for £2.10.

Sand was brought from Par to Fowey by horse and cart. A few individuals then got together to buy a lorry which was used to carry rubbish and sand etc. One man used to make concrete blocks on site for houses. 1934-5 we started to get concrete blocks from ECLP.

I've caught fish as a boy down on Polruan Quay and watch the plaice coming in on the sand. And we'd be in the boats with a bit of string looped around your finger and pull the one you want and twick em up and you'd get bags of 'em. We'd watch 'em come in when the tide coming in and they'd start comin' in. The harbour would be full of fish. Soon as you had this here new sump come out, soap powder and all that, and all this diesel - fish gone.

You look at Polruan Harbour you see a line right along. There'd be seaweed from there down, thick. You go down Polruan Quay, see it all up there on the wall, and it would be hanging off the wall. And summer evenings you'd have an old paint tin, and you'd tie a bit of limpet on a bit of string and put in over. And in the weed up the side of the quay - that's the weed with the poppers (i.e. bladder wrack) - you put a piece of limpet down, and we'd stay there all evening catching these crabs and putting 'em in a tin. And then we'd chuck 'em all in and catch them again tomorrow night. But this was our pastime. You had to amuse yourself all the time. They were shore crabs. You couldn't eat them.

But then you got lobsters come in the quay, you know on the slip in the end of the quay, and congers. I seen Captain Dow catch a great big conger, and they et everything they caught. Puck used to catch conger there regular underneath where the ferry came in. There's a hole there; and when it was very low tide, he'd catch this conger. He'd always say, "Conger in here!", and he had to get this conger, Puck would.. That was their little thing they had to do every time the tide was out.

They used to go shrimping up and down the shoreline and there used to be what we call green grass like grass. Seen it off Polmarine. When the tide would run out that would be covered. And they'd be out there shrimping through there - buckets of shrimp wa'n't it? You don't see it now. Yeah, up the river where there was no detergents chasin' it away. But most of the people went fishing in the evenings, you know, and would catch enough fish to keep mother and father going.

I've actually seen Looe men come in with their fishin' boats and tie up along the Quay and sell mackerel a bob a hundred. A bob a hundred, they was. And I've seen nets shot from there across to Jack Toms' yard, as you know, and they'd be catching mullet. And you'd go down the steps. And no lie, you could dip whitebait up by the bucket. But you don't see it now. No, cuz everything's fished out.

When the people made nets, they made it of string and tarred it; and it was hard work. But now they fishing with what they put on a rod now, very fine stuff. And nobody can't see it. Bloody ghost net down there. And if they lose they nets, they nets is there for years cuz they don't rot. They're still there, hundreds and hundreds of miles of it. And it's down on the bottom, and it won't move. Course it kill the fish, course it do. Yeah. That's what happens with 'em. These people find somethin' else, and pollutin' everything.

A couple of weeks ago somebody was coming up the Channel in a big ship, and there were all these fish floating down the river - about three mile of un. And these Spaniards had dumped them because they had over their quota. They wouldn't take 'em home; so they dumped them overboard. They ain't no good, no, but then, they couldn't take 'em home. It was in the news it was - miles of it floating down.

Now, we used to catch shads, di'n' us - any bugger can catch they. During the war all we had was shads. You could go out Punchy Cross and put a stone down with a weight on and catch these shad for a pastime. You could catch un on an old dirty rag, but they handsome fish wa'n't them? It tasted good, like a bream. They were like a little bream, very rough skins, very rough scales. And after the war finished we never saw any more. They were there during the war. I don't know what for, but out by the castle and along there all these little fish, like bream, rough; but they were ever so sweet little fish, not very big but very nice. And they disappeared. Never saw 'em any more. Queer, wasn't it?

See, that's why you see a lot of sailing ships in Fowey Harbour in they days. They come here for china clay and stuff like that. I can remember my father and they working on the docks, and they was shovelin' clay with big shovels in and out, and your talking about three or four hundred men working on the docks. Now they'm shifting more clay in a day than they shifted in twelve months. And how many's up there? Only about twenty, thirty men workin' there now. They've got dumpers there and push-button here and pushin' there. And they've got no work at all, see. My father used to come home. You couldn't see him for clay - his eyes, nose, ears, everything clay. Now they come home, you don't know they've been anywhere - all clean. They have changing rooms and shower rooms and all the rest of it. See, times have changed.

My father went up when he was about sixteen, and they said he was too young. So he went up again some years after. And he got injured up there with his arm and his leg; he got caught in the capstan. But he didn't have any compensation. They just graded him down to a C Class man, and he just had to use the capstan - you know the big wheel with the wire around - which had caused his accident in the first place.

But when he first went up there, they had big horses which brought the clay wagons in. And when it was frosty weather and icy, the sheets that covered the wagons over - they couldn't undo 'em. They had to cut the ropes because they were frozen solid. They'd stand up and look at you, a tall sheet of canvas which was over the wagons. It was terrible! All their fingers were chapped, they had great big cuts opened on their fingers, callouses on their hands, you never saw, like great warts all standing up on their hands. Terrible! No gloves! You had to supply all your own clothing in they days. The bloody socks they had on, they'd take they off and put 'em on their hands.

I don't suppose they possessed gloves in they days. Do you know, there was lots of things people di'n't have. You only bought things that were necessary, not luxuries. They didn't have no money for luxuries. Even me, I never had a pair of Wellington boots in my life nor a cardigan or any extra type of things. You only had what you needed to wear and what you needed to eat. Nothing was bought in the house unless there was a necessity. Don't buy no luxuries, di'n't have the money for it. You just had the bare essentials that you needed.

In the summer-time you go up the farmers, you know. You could go up up there and work. And you'd have the handsomest meals brought out to you, pasties, and buns, saffron buns - beautiful. They never paid no money. You could have a bag of spuds or take a couple of chicken or a bag of turnips. They never parted with no money, never. You could have somethin' but no money. That's how they were. You could go up there after the war, and you'd do all sorts. But you never got paid for it. Cuz I built a pigs' house for them out back. Never paid for un, but you could have a chicken. Yeah. Farmers never parted with any money, no. You could have it "in kind", as they called it.

There was no washing machines or anything like that. You had to boil the copper up out in the wash-house and a great big wooden tray, as they called it, like a big slope-sided wooden affair that you did your washin' in, and your mangle and everything. And it was a whole day's work anybody to do their washin'. There was a bowl for this and a bowl for that. There was a blueing bowl, and there was a starchin' bowl and everything like that, all different. And it took everybody all day to do it.

And some had a communal wash-house - down in Tom's yard they had a row of toilets and there was one wash-house, and this wash-house was shared by all - and each woman would take their washing, had to clean the place up and wipe it all down. And all the copper had to be cleaned out, all the fire and all had to be cleaned out for the next person. And each one had their day when they did it.

But lots of time I've looked at a photo and said, "Oh, it must be a wash day because all the lines in Polruan got their washin' out." On a Monday, all the lines hanging out all over Polruan. But that happened in a lot of courtyards. Over in his mother's courtyard and over in East Street behind that row of houses they had a communal wash-house and I think down on the wharf. And quite a lot of others all had communal wash-houses. Up in the court yard behind where Glynnis used to live in Fore Street, that had a communal wash-house and each one had a special place for washin'.

And a lot of ladies took in washing. A lot of shops didn't have any facilities, like Mrs. Peard's shop down on the corner there. Now Mrs. Braddon and Janie Hunkin used to take in their washin' for them. And you'd see these ladies all running around of an evening with a bundle of clean washing all ironed and pressed and everything with a big sheet of newspaper (cuz they didn't have wrappin' paper in those days, you know), all runnin' around in the evening with the washin', delivering to the people they did the washing for.

That's why they say these days about old grannies and that. Grannie smooths out all the paper and undoes all the string and picks up all the little bits. Because that was the way we was brought up. Nothin' was ever wasted. You had to save it. A piece of brown paper - you couldn't afford to go out and buy brown paper. But if a parcel came, you smoothed it all out and kept it.

We went to Fowey School when we were eleven or twelve and spent the whole Thursday learning housekeeping. We had to scrub, clean, do black-lead stoves, clean gas stoves, do cookin', grammar school cookin', for the day. We had to do their dinners. Then we had to clear out dinner time and go down in town. Then we had to come back again and carry on our cookin' in the afternoon. But we made cakes, general cooking, cleaned out cupboards, scrubbed tea-towels, hung 'em up all to dry on the things when we left over there, and everything. The wooden tables were all scrubbed with the grain and cleaned down after with cold water so the wood all came up. We had a good teacher over there - Miss Cumbley - and she kept us going all day.

When I left school I went to work for Lloyd Dunn and his wife. So I had five shillings a week, and she kept you going all day from nine o'clock in the morning till half past four in the afternoon. She found a job up until the last minute. And I was only fourteen then and five bob a week. I give mother half a crown, and I had half a crown. And I worked for her fer twelve month.

And then I went up to Wesley Bray, and I carried milk around twice a day, morning and evening. four gallons of milk I was carrying - two gallons in each hand and dipping it out as you went down the street to every house, up and down steps. And if it was frosty and I slid out on me backside' I had to hold on to the can cuz it was during the war. And I was afraid for my life I was going to lose the milk cuz there wasn't no more up the farm. What I had was what there was. And I had to go around again after tea, anywhere from five o'clock because some old dears would only have half a pint in the morning and another half in the evening cuz it was fresh. They didn't remember the dip was coming out of the milk you had spare. You had your half pint measure or pint measure whatever. And then I had to clean all the cans out, scrub 'em all out in boiling hot water, soda water. And I had 12/6 a week then up until I got married. And that was from the age of fifteen till I was twenty. And that was my lot until I got married.

And you had to do housework, cleaning, all sorts up there when I worked for Wesley Bray's mother. He lived up the next one to Mrs Pearce's, where Hamilton lives with Margaret. Mrs Bray was took bad, and she couldn't be left; so I had to sleep in up there. It was hard work. Mrs Butts was the last house there - there was a farm there. Mrs Butts was the last house in on the left hand side, but Westwinds was the last building on the right hand side across from Bunt's garage.

Can you imagine coming up to Lostwithiel and buying cows as a butcher, buying cows over here in the market and walk the buggers back to Polruan? They used to walk them back to Polruan . Wesley Bray had a lot them there. And take 'em in the fields like and used to kill 'em from there. That's how they had to do it. They was no lorries comin' with a load of meat. And where David Sandercock had his workshop, that was a killing. They used to go in a little gate in the side. That's why they walls is high; so they couldn't jump out over. And they used to go in through there and take 'em on the block, and that was that. I believe that block's still there. That's how things was done in they days. If a farmer wanted to take cows or something to market, he had to take them on foot. You know, if he wanted to come back from the market, he had to bring un in on his own. And they used to do miles in they days. They was all the same.

And come Christmas, you know, we had chicken. We never seen chicken all the year we was born, did us. We never had a chicken all our life, only at Christmas, when we were brought up. Well, chicken was a luxury. We had beef and lamb and a big marrow bone to make a nice bit of stew and that sort of thing, but never had chicken. Chickens had eggs. They wouldn't kill chicken. They was free running then.

When I come home after the war, we went away on a farm and did a job fer some old boy. And I asked, "Got any eggs mister?"

"No, we haven't seen a egg for years. Can't understand it." So...I had a ladder up against the hayrack where they used to cut the hay to feed the cows 'n that - they cut it with a knife. And all these eggs was up there on top. So I had a blue pencil, and I marked them all. And the next day they that wasn't marked, they was mine. God, capers we used to have!

Jack Turner would be up the ladder. "Hey, there's whackum up here today."

I'd say, "Pass 'em all down."

There again, people used to say to me, "Did you ever go up Pelynt?"

"Pelynt," I said, "it's bloody miles away!" We never had no meat to kill in Pelynt. We didn't know where it was to anyway.

I never went to Polperro till after I was married, never, never went to Polperro. And then I went in the dark cuz we went with the ladies' choir, and so I couldn't see anything. I've been many times since. But I mean, I was twenty when I got married, and that's the first time I'd ever been to Polperro.

My father used to walk there when they were boys and go down after the girls you know, and get chucked in the river down there by the Polperro men cuz they didn't want them down there after the girls. My father used to tell me that. But they didn't like you coming and poaching on their preserves at all. In the stream down there if you set foot down there. But you didn't go nowhere because you had to walk, you see. And so that was a deterrent to start with. Several used to go with horse and trap. And they would have about ten goin' on a wagonette. Well, we come to a hill, they had to get out and walk. Soon as they go up a hill, they had to walk up a hill and right down.

But then you was just happy playing on the quay on the beach, or up watching the sail, and chasing up in the hills, goin' round and doin' things to other poor old devils.

There was a shop out past Mr Freeman's where Denzil used to live, the next shop on from there. Keelson. Marines were there during the war stationed. They had a contingent of marines there, all English, staying there. But when my father was young, it was old Charlie Stephens' shop, and he sold anything. And my father and a crowd of boys would get in. And they'd have him up and down the steps, gettin' the bottles of sweets down. And they all wanted a ha'penth of whatever. Well, they'd keep him up and down the steps, and each one would want what he'd put up before, and so he was up and down the steps.

But once they'd left the shop, they'd have a bit of cotton on the doorbell. And they would go along and up Sidney Hill, you know, Tinkers Hill, out of sight and pull on the cotton. And the doorbell would be ringing, you see. And he'd come out, but he couldn't see nobody. And he couldn't see the cotton cuz it was so fine. They had all sorts of games like that - always pinchin' something from somewhere or playing games on somebody.

And then I wasn't home (from the war) a week before I started to work again. Laurie Bray wanted a job done, and he come and asked me to do a job for un. Ethel Bray's husband.

In the meantime he would be taking gentlemen out to their yachts and have a few shillings during the Regatta during the evening when you were there at the fun fair. Beside the Town Quay, you see, they used to hold water polo there, regular water polo there. Yeah, very nice they were. They used to have nets out from here in a square, and all the boats would be around the edge - that's before the war. Out here would be the water polo. And you'd have all the water polo matches from St Austell and all the surrounding places who had a water polo team and come and play the team of Fowey. And whoever had a rowing boat like you see all these here, they would all come around the edge the perimeter and stand up and cheer and everything. It was lovely.

In gig races they used great long oars of ash which bent like a bow. They ran lines down the river alongside all day; so people couldn't go out and interrupt the races.

FRED TALLING
BORN IN 1928, SPEAKING IN 1996

I was born at Trenewen in Lansallos, but I grew up at Trevedda, in Lanteglos. Then we lived at Highway and then moved to Churchtown Farm. Father was a tenant of Trevedda, owned by Boconnoc Estate. My brothers were John, Tom, and Gerald. My sisters were Elsie and Florence.

I went to school at Whitecross. My brothers were older and went to Pelynt School when we lived at Trenewen. They had over a three mile walk every day. There used to be a steam lorry which worked on the roads, and sometimes they got a lift on that. I don't expect it went much faster than them walking. They carried their dinner to school every day - pasties, egg sandwiches, etc.

Whitecross School had three teachers before the war, then two during the war, then three again when the evacuees came from Bristol with their teacher. The headmaster, "Skip" was a lazy old devil. He didn't do much work and didn't make we do much either - that was our trouble.

Once Bernard Roseveare had two bangers near Guy Fawkes Day. He lit one on the school steps, then another. The first one went off, and Skip came out, then the other went off nearly under his feet.

Three or four of us used to go to Fowey half a day a week for carpentry. The girls went for cookery if they wanted to, but on a different day, not the same day as we - they didn't allow that to happen.

The biggest change in farming came when tractors came in 1935. Before, it was steam and horses. The thrashing machine was owned by contractors - two men; the engine driver and the man who fed the sheaves into the machine. No one had tractors around here in the First World War. Then old Fred Mutton, a carpenter at Penpol, had a Fordson tractor to work the saw bench. And Bryant, the other side of Lanreath at Botallick, had an Overtime tractor used mainly to drive the machinery for thrashing and milling. In those days tractors weren't good for steering or braking. After, when better ones came in about 1935, then they were used in the fields. A lot of them, then, were American.

Well, in about five years everything changed. It was because of Harry Fergusen. He brought in his Fergusen tractors with hydraulic lifts; and once they got that workin', you couldn't compete. It was a marvellous invention, to be quite honest. You see, inventions, hydraulics, tractors, and these great diggers that lift ten to twenty tons - it all came out of his idea.

And some of the blokes who used to maintain farm machinery, blacksmiths, they used to shoe horses. In them days, see, a lot of old machinery was - I mean, now it's all boughten parts. In them days they made them. Blacksmiths, they put on another piece with your harrows. They'd fire and join on another piece and make them new again. That's how it worked in them days. Now when something's wore out, they send them away. Blacksmith used to shoe horses, but then the Furgusen tractors come in with all that new equipment. It more or less knocked a lot of people out of business, really, cuz all boughten parts came in.

In the winter we brought in the fat cattle and young ones and sometimes cows if it was very cold. We'd bring cows in to calve. The barn used to have stalls, one to a stall. We fed them on mangles and turnips and hay. Once in a while we might mix in some peas, but they were hard to thrash. We grew all the feed on the farm, didn't buy in feed. There was ground barley for pigs, and we bought "sharps", fine wheatens, husks left from the flour. And we fed them swill - peelings and cabbage. The pigs were shut in to fatten, but the sows ran around the yard - they'd come in the back door if you let them. To stop them rooting in the fields, we'd "spookum" - put rings in their noses. They'd have the whole field up else. Chickens would run around the yard too. We'd throw out a dipper of corn to them each day, and pick up the eggs wherever we could find them. Sometimes we'd find a pile in the straw we'd missed.

Butchers came around to the farms and bought fat cattle. Ours used to go to Polperro and Lerryn - there were four butchers in Lerryn at one time. We tried to get cattle sold soon after Christmas to get a good price. Course, in them days, the butchers, when they wanted a pig, a sheep, or a lamb, they would come around and generally kill them on the farm and carry them home in their vans. They never had all these great big abattoirs in them days. Same with the pigs - they were always killed on the farm. A lot of times they had to slaughter on the farm and carry them home in their pony and trap, and they'd skin them back at their place. Hard times on the farms in them days. Course, you didn't ask the Ministry bloke for anything then, just sold 'em off.

We kept big long wool sheep, South Devons, sometimes crossed with Suffolk rams to get the black face. They were shorn with ordinary shears. Then father had power clippers. One man turned the handle rather fast while the other sheared the sheep. You had to turn fast to make the clippers work well. Then the old fashioned Lister petrol machines came in to drive the clippers - ran two clippers off one engine. Lister were the main producers of clippers then. We lambed outdoors unless we brought one in, out of the cold, that was about to lamb. We never had a house for the whole flock.

There were not too many vets around - the nearest one was at Liskeard. It had to be something very serious to call in the vet - not a cow or anything - had to be a horse or something, the main work horse. Horses got colic; and if one did, you had to lead him around and not let him lie down and get the vet pretty quick. When they came in hot from the field, they weren't to drink too much water. A good horse was expensive, perhaps £50, a lot of money then.

We had two shire horses, Duke and Darling, and one lighter one for the farm cart. The farm cart was two-wheeled and would tip for carrying roots etc. It could carry half a ton if you could get it in - enough for a horse. Two horses were used for a hill. The chain horse went in front and helped the cart up the hill. Then once it was on the level one horse would take it - easier to control; and a school girl or school boy would take the chain horse back down the hill for the next load.

We didn't have a trap; we used a bicycle. If Father was going to Lostwithiel market, he'd cycle to Fowey, then take the train up. Elsie, my older sister, walked cattle home from Lostwithiel. Then cattle lorries started coming in. Old Dick Carnall used to take a brood of little pigs to Lostwithiel market every week in his cart, which was bigger than a trap but not so big as a farm wagon. He was a bit of a cripple and went around the farm on a horse. He had a stick to lift the latches on the gates. We didn't go to Liskeard market; it was too far. There was a cattle market at Looe in them days, too, up by the station.

When Frank Ball lived at Trethake Mill, he used to go up Liskeard and buy a lot of pigs. My brother and his friends used to do gardening at Coomland at that time, and the pigs would come in the garden and eat all their crops. They couldn't do anything to stop it. Well, Frank Ball used to have a fair lorry, in them days, delivering coal, binder twine - agricultural sundries, you'd call it. So they thought they'd stop'un letting his pigs run all over. They waited until they heard the lorry, then waited till just before he came, then frightened the pigs out of the garden in front of his lorry. Well, the pigs went under the lorry, everywhere; but damned if he didn't touch one. They thought if he killed one, he wouldn't let them run free. But it did no good - he didn't change.

There was an old saying of the millers. Old Frank Ball knew this old saying. Well, one day a bloke came up to him and said the old saying; "They tell me that an honest miller grows hair on the palms of his hands."

Frank Ball said, "Oh yes, it's very true. You're right there."

So the bloke says to Frank Ball, "Let's have a look at your hands. I can't see any hair on the palms of your hands."

Old Ball says, "Well, only an honest miller can see 'un!"

The earliest harvests I can remember, the harvest was done with horses and binder. Father can remember doing it with the scythe delivery rake, pulled by horse. You went along and cut the corn. Every once in a while the rake would put the cut corn into a sheaf, then men came along and tied it into a sheaf with a bit of straw. They could do it very quickly. The sheaves were carried into rows by hand, and men would shock them - put seven to nine into a stack with one in the middle, the others leaning in around it (tepee shaped). Local road men and others - Garth Rollings, the blacksmith from Pont, and different ones helped in the evenings. We were glad of their help. Women helped, carrying sheaves and the like. Miss Fox used to come and help in the War (she's Mrs. Michael in Lerryn now). She used to live in Readymoney. Alice Talling (1) used to travel with the threshing machine in the War. Two land girls would go with it.

Thrash day was a big day on the farm. Farmers helped each other thrashing in winter. It was "borrow-lend" men. It took eleven men to do a day's thrashing. The day before, we had to draw water and coal for the steam engine, which would use six or seven hundredweight and a hell of a lot of water. We had to cart it out to the field - we took a tank out and carried the water out in barrels on the cart to fill the tank.

Thrash days were busy for the women. They always gave the men dinner. The men on the threshing machine would come from the next farm about nine in the evening after they had done a day's work there, and have supper - ham and fried potatoes. Then they'd go home for the night and come about six in the morning and have breakfast - farm bacon, eggs, etc. The whole gang would come about nine after feeding their own animals etc. at home. Dinner time, the farmer's wife and other women in the house (or if none she got some in to help) cooked a big dinner for all the men - chicken pies, big ham, roast pork - all home grown. Mother had my sisters, Elsie and Flo, to help. In the war we were allowed to kill two pigs a year, but we had to give up our bacon ration coupons. Elsie married Albert Kinver. His father, Tom Kinver, used to drive a thrashing machine owned by Sussex at Lanreath, who owned three thrashing sets and two steam engines.

Used to be, when lambs were two or three months old, you'd go out with a big butchers knife, catch the lamb by the tail, and of course the lamb would try to pull away, and they'd cut his tail off. They never had no treatment for bleeding or anything. And then they'd take these tails, save them all, and they'd go in and skin them out then. And when they was skinned out, they was about, oh, smaller than your finger, just like a ordinary rat's tail once the skin was taken. And then they'd fry them all up. I didn't fancy them. We didn't do that actually, but that's what most farmers did. And that was wonderful food. I don't know how they ate them. They used to fry 'em. I suppose you'd pick them between your teeth and leave the bones, I don't know.

This was how they do in them days. They would bleed quite a bit when they cut the tails off you know. You wouldn't be allowed to cut off lambs tails like that nowadays. And lambs is better if you don't cut them too short. But you gotta do it else they get maggots. I've got two or three long tail sheep in there now, and they'm the worst ones I've got for gettin' maggots, you know. I don't cut off lambs tails now because they've gone to factory before you need to bother. And it checks them growing; so I don't bother. They're all gone for slaughter in four months.

This (at Highway) was a little farm at one time. The chap used to keep horses and a few cows. He had some in the field down past Lawhippet, there. He was called Steed. I can't remember him, but I remember - I suppose it was his wife or sister, Mary Steed. She used to live here, I remember that. But it was before that that this chap used to keep these horses. And he used to go along and hire these horses if you wanted some stones carted, or whatever. And he used to go off and do it for people. They used to keep two or three cows and sell the cream and butter. And that used to be out where the garages are. And he used to keep pigs as well. I think he might have rented some land out that way, but I think Leslie said he rented some off Lawhippet, which is out on the point out there. But they also owned two fields down here, as well. The garages, just what belongs to the house here, that was the stables and the cow house, you know. You can still see the crooks - they have bits of chain up on the beams now where they used to hang the pig when they killed it. It's still out there, that is, hanging up on the beam.

A chap called Billy Willcocks used to lodge here with Mrs. Steed. That was a long time ago. He didn't used to get too much to eat some days, you know. And she was always terrible upset if a hen was eatin' an egg. She'd have her killed, you know. Well, you see, if you break the egg first and put it in, any hen will go and eat it, won't they? When Billy used to get hungry, he'd crack an egg. All the hens would be runnin' out. He'd nip in, "Mrs Steed, quick! Your hen is eatin' the egg!"

"Kill it, Billy, kill it, Billy! He'd have to kill the chicken. He used to chop her head off. That would stop it. That was true. That's what he used to do.

Another thing he used to do - they had a chaff cutter. You know the chaff cutter - in the old days you'd turn the handle; it would cut up the straw up in little pieces for the horses. It'd be hard work turning the handle. Billy'd be shovellin' in the straw. When he got fed up with it, he'd stick the fork in. That'd break the fork - he couldn't do any more that day till he got a new handle.

143

My grandfather, actually, he was a bit of a temperamental sort of bloke. If he said something wa'n't right, it wa'n't right. But he could sometimes be wrong now and then. Father said when he was young, they had a chap working for him. They had a beautiful field of hay. It was lovely and fit for carryin' - they used to carry it in a rick in them day or else with horses and wagons. They went out and looked, my father and this young chap that was helpin'. They went in and told my grandfather, "That hay is beautiful. It's fit for carryin' in."

So then my grandfather has to go out. So Father said they went out and got lookin' at this hay. And my grandfather said "This hay is no more fit to carry in than I'm fit to go to hell," he said.

The young boy looked at him and said, "Let's carry it right in then!"

Another time the same chap was working with Father, and of course they weren't very well off in those days. An old tramp come to buy rabbit skins. He had a damned great bag full of skins, you know. So he and my father looked in the hayhouse, and the tramp was in there asleep with all the skins. And so they two pinched so many skins from the tramp's bag. So the chap waited and waited. And then he seen the old tramp leavin'; and he said, "I gotta few skins I could sell you, you know." He did. Father said he sold him his own bloomin' skins. The old tramp never cottoned on - amazing. Yeah, that was a true story, really, it happened.

Another time, over at Leslie's uncle's, over at St Cadox, an old chap used to stay around there. And he used to sleep in the straw at night.

"Let's go down with a light with a gun 'n see if we can shoot rats." He looks in the barn. The bloomin' rat was going across; so they shot, "Bang" at the rat! Out jumps this chap! He was in there asleep, and he came out a hollerin' and swearin'. But they never hit him anyway. Frightened them as well, I think. It was true. These things really happened, not made up.

There used to be a chap down Polruan called Charlie Thomas who used to go around the farms selling fruit. The Honeys used to farm at Castle or Mixtow farm. Well, Charlie Thomas went down to this farm. There was a little pig running around, a runt or "nestlebird" as we called them. Anyway old Charlie Thomas went down to the farm, and Honey said, "If you can catch that little nestlebird you can have it. So he caught it and put it in a sack.

Now near Whitecross, Charlie met Honey the farmer's son, who saw the sack moving and could see something was in it. "I'll give you five shillings for what's in your sack," he said.

So Charlie said, "All right." No sooner than he said that, then Honey knew he'd been had. He'd bought his own pig back. He didn't dare take it back home again to his father. So he hit it over the head and threw it away.

We used to go to Rolling's Fair at the quay in Fowey. Then it moved up to the top park because I think someone fell off the swing boats into the river. Anyhow it was hard for the steam engines to get down to the Quay.

Well, the cinema started at Fowey, di'n't it? Near Berril's yard first. We used to go there Saturday night. We used to go there and cross the Bodinnick Ferry. And then we used to go around in different gangs like. We didn't go too much to the pub, didn't have enough money to go very much. They could get cider free. My father, he never paid anybody anything. You had to work for your keep, actually, but we was allowed to go out rabbiting, as we called it, catch some rabbits to sell. 'N they'd give you some money sometimes; You never got no wages. That happened on all the farms, no wages. You was hoping that he would set you up on a farm when old enough. But with four boys, it was very difficult.

We used to keep ferrets and do a lot of rabbiting and things like that. Not just for the profit of the rabbits - we used to enjoy doin' it, you know. Fishing, anything that wouldn't cost a lot. We went out on the cliffs, mainly Lantivet Bay. Sometimes trout down in the river. Used to have trout down in the mill stream, used to have nice trout there, Pont right up to Trethake, you know. We'd catch some. I don't know, they seem to have gone now. Whether it's silage, I looked the other day, couldn't see one. You'd think there'd still be some, wouldn't you? I think it's the slurry, if anything. They're more careful than they were; but I saw the other day, on the tele, they had a big do again on one of the farms letting silage and slurry in the rivers. Terrible thing, i'n' it, when it do get in the river.

Before the war you used to, if you had the farm and didn't want to catch the rabbits yourself, you could sell the rights to those rabbits for one year for one winter to a season. Trapper, whatever he caught was his - he'd get a livin' off of them. They had all these gins which is banned now, as you know. Some of them had two to three hundred gin traps. Some days they'd catch a hundred, two hundred rabbits, and that's how they kept them under control.

Most of them chaps who was trappers would help on the farm when the thrashin' machines came. They'd have seen to their traps, done all that, early in the morning. Then they'd do a day's work for the farmer, thrashin'; and they'd get a bit extra that way, you know. But there was a hell of a lot of poaching each other's rabbits, these trappers. They had great big dogs goin' out rabbiting, all that sort of thing, and go in someone else's field and get half a dozen - that was a bonus, really. But that always happened. They used greyhounds, mostly, whippets and that. The rabbits, they used to breed and come back. Though, really, it was a cruel way of catchin' the poor rabbits, gettin' them in these traps, really. But they had to do something to keep them down. Some birds, like partridges and that, used to get caught; and cats used to get caught in them. There wasn't so many foxes in those days. Whether the trappers kept 'em down or no, I don't know. Didn't see many foxes around here, then. Now there is.

They used to have a rabbit man come around every day to pick up these rabbits. One of them was called Tonkins, from Looe. They had a little lorry, and they used to have bars all the way across this lorry. And they'd leg two rabbits together - you've seen that, call it a brace. And they used to put them all along these bars. And when it was Christmas time, and everybody been catching rabbits; they had a whole lorry load of rabbits. And the price was controlled by the Ministry.

They killed the rabbit by wringing its neck, sometimes a couple of hundred of a morning. Some rabbits wa'n't it really? Used to eat the corn, the beggars would. But out on Triggabrowne hills they used to trap most, because they'd come up all the way from the bottom of the fields up top. And then they lay the traps all along where the grass field started, and they'd get hundreds of bloomin' rabbits coming up there.

We used to get Gipsies coming around, genuine ones. They'd bring their clothes pegs and pinch a few rabbits out of the field. They used to ask Father if they could put their ponies in the field for the night. I don't think he ever got paid for it, maybe a few coppers. They never used to say anything about curses or nothing. It was mainly the Crocker family.

We also had knife grinders and scissor grinders, and tradespeople coming. Midnight Harry was a baker from Looe who used to come to Trevedda. He'd arrive about ten-thirty at night. He used to drink cider on the way and used to get a bit tiddly at times. He came in a van with a great big basket of bread and packets of yeast. Mother didn't buy cakes - she made her own. I've never seen a man who could make a cigarette so quick with his finger.

A bloke called Glanville and his son came once a year to mend the harness. They were saddlers from Wadebridge. He'd sell saucepans and shot gun cartridges as well. He was the cleverest bloke I've ever seen, stitched it all by hand, used to flock the collar for the horses - put straw inside and then lovely soft material. It was beautiful and was renewed every year. When we were kids, we used to ask him for a pair of leather bootlaces. He'd be so clever - he'd take out his knife and, swish, cut them from a wide piece of leather just like that. He mended binder canvases too. He was really skilled. In the old days Father said they used to spend the night when they came by horse, but I remember they had an old Trojan van.

We used to have a tailor, Harvey, come from Marshalls at Bodmin. He'd just look at you and say "I have a coat would fit you." Or "I have a suit would fit you". It would, too. He could tell just by looking at us.

We used to have a lot of tailors that used to come around. If you wanted a new suit, you didn't have to go to a shop. They'd come and size you up. Here's a suit for you, sort of thing. Sometimes they brought one with them, cost about £3, or else they made to measure which would cost a bit more. They had lovely patterns, always carried patterns. You see, in them days, if there was a wedding or a funeral - if it was a funeral, the woman used to go and get special black clothes. As soon as a tailor heard that somebody died, he be there the same day or the next day to see what they needed to go to the funeral. That was his job, really. If there was a wedding, he'd be on as well.

My uncle was a tailor, you know, in Lostwithiel. He used to make suits, that sort of of thing. I'll tell you why he learnt to be a tailor. He had a club foot, had a extra big boot on the foot for some reason. He thought if he learnt that, he would be more or less sitting down - better than outdoors. He done very well out of it, I think, yeah. Everyone was struggling in those days, though. They say they're struggling now, but in the Twenties. The Thirties was the worst, I think. I can't remember the Twenties, but in the Thirties...

On the farms at Polruan they didn't used to produce much grain, no more than a couple of fields. Mr. Pearce's was a bigger farm but the others was just dairy, like, a small milk round, about eight cows, like Mr. Bray and "Officer" Crapp. They always called him Officer. Mr. Crapp, he was a nice old chap, he was. He always had a saying about anything - it was always a "circular curibulum", if he was talkin' about anything. He was a nice man. He used to farm Essa.

And then, Cyril Libby would be at Pont. He used to keep a few cows. He had a milk round in Polruan as well. He used to have a motor bike and side car to take the milk in, had a churn with a cap on it and measure it out as they go.

Dick Carnall used to make cider at Yeate Farm at one time. And after he left, Mr. Devonshire took over and farmed it.

The Balls were at Trethake for years. "Canon" Ball we called him. When they sold the rectory at Lansallos, he went and bought it, yeah; and he lived up there. And he was runnin' the mill as well. And he had a chap worked for him called Sid Luke...so we used to call them "Canon" Ball and "Disciple" Luke. He's dead now, Sid Luke. A great beekeeper, he was.

Sid used to see to picking the millstones, they used to called it. They had to chip the granite so it would be rough to grind corn. They used to make a track in the stone. It would be thick at one end and then they'd come down to a smaller size; so as the corn went through, it got finer down through, down through the end of the stone and fall down into the hopper like. Some apple mills had some of the same principle, only round the other way like a roller with granites. But they went round with a millstone with a flat place. They used to have to pick them out fairly often because it would wear away rubbing together. I suppose everybody who had so much flour had so much granite.

Mr. Devonshire, Francis Devonshire, was at Lawhippet first. And then he went to down to Yeate. And after Mr. Devonshire went down to Yeate, a man called Ernie Mutton was at Lawhippet. He had a milk round Bodinnick way at one time. And he used to grow a lot of plants to sell - salad, broccoli, flat ball cabbage, and any type of plants he used to sell. He used to sell them around to farmers and different people. I think he was a gardener before he went farming, had a fair knowledge of how to do that sort of thing. You could get so much more money per acre. Course, you gotta put a lot of work into it. But you can get a lot of money.

At Trevarder the first one I can remember was a man called Ernie Searle. I don't know how long he was there. He must have been there a long time before I can remember. He used to make rhubarb wine, and that was terribly strong. I remember when we used to go around to parties at Christmas, he always used to bring it. And we used to go down Mr. Lemon's. And another man called Mr. Libby - that would be

Ronald Libby's father - used to live at Coomland then, and they used to have these parties. The old men played the concertina in them days, and Mr. Lemon could play. He used to play somethin' as well - tambourine - and they used to make nice music, used to dance to it. Parties would be held in the house. I wasn't very old then. Everyone used to go. Tons to eat, best you could get. I expect they had enough to last them a week after.

A man called Collings was at Triggabrown. He was always in a hurry. He had a tractor 'n cart. Always in a rush. He also had a farm in the war down at Pennytinny, down St. Columb way, or somewhere, as well. Chap used to work for him lived in the house - he ran the farm for him. When he gave up, he came back to Polruan to live - in that house that Mr Butts' got at Townsend.

And in the war there was an old chap from Plymouth down here at Carne Farm, you know; and he made up the road from Carne farm to Pont by digging out the shard. You know what it was called - soil when it gets stone in it - shellet, you know, is what they call that shaley stone. Don't know how many tons of shellet he dug. And everybody nicknamed him "Shellet". And he reared a bull, you know, for John Lemon up there, and he took it around to markets and shows and all sorts of things. And he had a daughter, and she was a little bit glamourous. And every young farmer used to go up there and see how they could get on .

Mr. Roseveare, at Frogmore, was the first one to have a dipping pool in this area for sheep. And all the farms from Lansallos all around in this area, all took sheep there. And they'd be dippin' sheep for about four or five days, you know, several thousand sheep. And that was when sheep dippin' came in first, when it was compulsory. And he was the only one to have a pool that could do it. We used to drive our sheep along the roads to get there, and he used to dip them all himself. He was a skilled man, really.

He used to keep a nice lot of cattle, South Devon. And he used to go down the beach and pick up lots of things in the war, you know, each day, see what was washed in, go down and get it. I was down there one day, and the Army had been and had put barbed wire along the cliffs to keep the Germans from coming up over, see. They had bits of barbed wire the Army had issued to them, see. I was down there going to go fishing, and I found one all in the brambles, a brand new loop of wire. I was comin' up with this wire on my back, an' I said, "You ought to go down there 'n have one or two of these."

He always called me Freddie Boy. "Old Freddie Boy, don't worry about it. I had the lorry up. They had a load," he said. "They unloaded a lot in my barns!" Well, that's one up on me, anyway. "Yeah," he said, "Freddie Boy, they'm unloaded in my barns."

Interesting old chap, he were, marvellous for sharpening saws or any tool, doing up engines or anythin'. He had a wonderful knowledge of things, he did. But then, I can't remember his father. But my father can remember him.

We were playing football one day. 'Gloucester City', a big ship in them days, was in the harbour under Prime Cellars when a German plane came over and tried to bomb it. The Germans were the only ones to have three engine planes, ours were two engines or four engines. They dropped four bombs, but they didn't hit it. We watched and saw shells being shot three or four times from Fowey at ships, but the plane was too high, out of range.

We used to pick blackberries, just for ourselves. I like blackberry and apple tart. My mother used to make a lot of plum jam, damson jam. I was never that keen on it. There's another name for a damson, i'n't there? And that grows a bit bigger than a damson.

I think in the war you was allowed a bit extra sugar or somethin' if you was to make jam. But a lot of beekeepers used to get sugar. Sometimes they didn't use it all, 'n then we'd have some of that - had to do the best you could in them days.

Farmin' was profitable in the war because there was such a demand fer everything, you know. There wasn't enough labour, really; but you used to manage sometimes an hour or two. Sometimes you couldn't get enough fertilizer you needed and things like that. They used to control how much you could have. And you was forced to grow so many potatoes. You had to; the Ministry made you.

In the war we had a lady - don't know if you call her a land girl or not - a lady called Miss Fox from Fowey. Mary used to manage Lawhire Farm; and Pamela - that's her sister- she used to come up Trevedda to help. But I don't think she ever got paid fer doin' it; she just used to come to help. And they live at Lerryn now. She worked for us for two or three year. Nice person, she was. She could milk cows as well. You had to be very careful then because, well, she was more particular than these rough and ready sorts.

I know that we were thrashing there one day, and she had corduroy trousers on, same as the men used to wear in them days - popular they were. And a mouse ran up her leg. She was there sputterin', screamin' for someone to help; but they couldn't. That's true.

When we was harvesting, what we was all waiting for, was refreshments. Pasties sometimes, and then apple tart and cream, bread and butter - homemade butter, splits, anything that they could pack easy to carry. Oh, and homemade buns - plain buns, I call 'em, saffron sometimes. But they couldn't get the saffron in the war so easy. Plain buns with caraway seeds. If you could get any currants, they would do some of those. You had to make do with what you could get, in them days. We drank tea mostly, yeah. You could get a bottle of cider; but if you drank that, it wasn't much good for workin' on, you know. But tea was the best thing of all, and we used to have it. Even when it was cold, it was nice. They'd make it all in a big kettle or anything you could carry. Mother used to have a big kettle to bring it out in, a great big market basket of food. It was nice!

We used to have extra helpers, lots of people, come in the evenings. They used to love to come 'n have somethin' to eat out of the basket. Course they used to have ham as well - ham -sandwiches. Some days it would be egg and bacon pies. Couldn't get much beef to make pasties very often. It was rationed.

You was allowed to kill two pigs a year on farms. Well anyone was allowed to, any household, you know, and that used to help out. But it was all salted bacon, hams. It was good. Their hams would keep two year if you wanted them to. Hung them up on beams, wrap 'em up newspaper, in paper, and then in a very tight bag. Put them in that, else you might get a fly blowin' up. And if you got a maggot, it would finish it. We used to have to salt it in brine in a trundle - that's a trough. Some people used half a cider barrel for it. We used to have a big granite trough.

After the war a little plane, a Sea Otter twin engine, came down in Trevedda. It was not a crash landing as such - it skimmed over along the ground, its belly pushing the earth ahead. Then it tipped over upside down. We ran over and thought it would catch fire, for it was some hot. But it didn't catch fire. There were three of them in the plane; the pilot, then another, then a Commander climbed out. The pilot said to the Commander," I hope we didn't frighten you."

"It would take more than that to frighten me!" he said.

Men stood guard till they took the petrol out. Some job it was, too, because the petrol was in the wings. They cut the pipe in the wings, and had a stick to put in when they wanted to. They filled up all Father's cans. It was high octane, a bit strong for cars; but they did it. When one of the officers from the airport down West came, he said, "I thought it was full of petrol."

The chaps guarding it said, "Well, it were, but people come to look, and was smoking; so we drained it away." They guarded it all night in the corn field. Then a crane came and lifted it over the hedge into a transporter. Father got paid for the damaged corn and a gate post that the crane broke.

Electricity didn't come to farms or Highway till about 1947-48. There were generators at Carneggan and Pendower, but they were only powerful enough for lights, not fridges or anything.

My mother and they used to have lot of milk go sour - never had refrigerators in those days. That was the biggest problem, just keeping things. It was a job, though, to keep any food. When I was a boy they called 'em safes - that was a cupboard with that very fine gauze - zinc - keep the flies out, and air could go in, and you could keep it a bit longer. I know farmers used to put their milk churns in the river, di'n' they, sometimes, if they was lucky enough to have a stream to cool it. It would keep 'em lovely 'n cool.

There was Tremeer. A man called Kelly had it, Brice Kelly he was called. And he farmed it right up till my father took it over in the War sometime. He died, actually; and his widow carried it on for a time. And then she packed it in. They used to have cider over there, as well. I don't know that they actually made it there. They made it at Lanlawren. But they grew the apples there, and they used to keep cider there. They had a big millpond. The spring wasn't enough to keep the water wheel going; so they had a big pond - let it build up and then released it over the wheel.

A lot of the farmers around then didn't bother to sell cider very much. A lot of 'em just made it for the men and themselves. And they would sell off some, you know; but they didn't do too much of that. The bigger ones, some of them, might. In St Veep some sold it. Mr. Devonshire used to, when he was down Lawhippet, because he had a nice orchard down there.

The Pearces have been at Trevecca as long as I can remember. Joey Pearce was there first. They used to grow a lot of apples, but they wouldn't have cider. And Roy's grandfather, Joey Pearce, he was terrible against smoking. When you smoked, he'd say, "When you smoke, you have a chimney in your neck!" But there was only one man was allowed to smoke in his house. That was Uncle Tom Mutton - used to be Captain of the 'Waterwitch' years ago. Joey Pearce said, "He's the only man allowed to smoke in this house for the simple reason I can't stop him."

Tommy used to say, "I used to go over, sit so close to him as I could."

At Christmas they'd go around the farms carol singing, things like that, yeah. Darkey Parties, they used to call them. They used to go around where there was cider on the farm. They only used to go around - they never collected for anything. They used to plan where 'e was going, about three farms in an evening. Course, they'd get all tight before the evening was out, had to go home, lost their way, all sorts of things.

They used to blacken their faces, you know, put on funny hats. Course, the farmers' wives were expecting them to come, in a way. And to make sure, they used to make all these big saffron cakes fer Christmas, special ones, didn't they? They used to call them Christmas cakes, but they were just the saffron cake, really. But they'd be annoyed if you didn't taste their saffron cakes, in them days. They have about, oh, seven or eight, made all ready for Christmas, of course. They'd keep fer quite a while, you see. They used to go and have their saffron cake and cider. And then they'd sing some carols as well. And then, when they'd have enough, they'd go on to the next farm. Always had a Darkey Party. I can just remember John and Tommy used to go to Jack Pearce's house, have their cider over there; and they was always expecting them. That's right, anyone who worked on the farm joined in. People worked on the docks would join in, and they'd go around together. I think Lanreath area was even more for that than around here.

I've heard Leslie Mutton say they used to have what he called a tea fight, but that was down at the Chapel. All of them used to go fer tea or somethin' down in a field. It was a Chapel Anniversary or somethin'. You see, kids in them days - there wasn't much entertainment. They would go out and think it was lovely for them.

Yeah, we had a mew steed in Trevedda until we had a big shed put up to keep the corn. And they had one at Tremeer. There were several around, but gradually they disappeared after a time. They were practical; but it meant you had to pitch your loads of corn a lot higher off your wagon cuz the staddle stones for the mew steed were about two foot six high. And then you had a big pole which went across that way. And then you had little poles going the other way for them to rest on.

And they'm up that high before you start your rick, you see. That meant when you got on a wagon, you had to pitch them up a hell of a height, you know. A mew was made up each end to a point. Some was made cone shape up country but not down here. We used to do them almost the shape of a house, you know, oblong like that and then a peaked roof like that, on top of the staddle stones, yeah.

Then you had to thatch them after that, you know, to keep the wet out, you see. I could thatch anyway. We used to have great long wooden ladders - they used to call them a spar, same as they have for the mast of a ship. And they'd split 'em back in two. And then they'd put the staves - (rungs) - we used to call it staves in they days. You'd start about this width, and then you'd gradually go in (tapered). They ladders 'd be in one piece, you know. Wouldn't be like the modern ones in three bits, you know. All in one piece. You had a heck of a job to bend that one up, as we used to call it. It was on the ground. You had to stick the bottom in the rick against somethin', and then go back to the end, and start and walk forward, pushin' un gradually. And when 'e got so high, then when 'e got the balance, it was all right - the weight was gone then. Once you got 'un on the rick, you used to just turn 'em over the mowhay.

Thatchin' - they used to make spears or spars, you know. You have a nut hole stick, hazel, but we used to always call it nut hole. And you'd go down in the woods, and you'd find all the young ones that was growin'. And that would be the size you use for a bean stick, about as big as your thumb, a bit bigger 'n that. Then you'd have a sharp hook - I don't know what you call un, a billhook or somethin'. And you'd split that one you kept on your knees. And then you'd split un right along, and you'd split it in half. Then you'd take that half and split in back again, and he'd be in quarters. And you'd get four sticks like for thatchin' out of that one. Then what you had - they had to be really sharp - and then hold 'un on your knee, and you could just sharpen the two ends like this, spearhead, we called it.

And then while they were still green and fresh, you had to twist them, and that was - you had to catch and turn 'em in your hands. And then one piece would be long and one short; and when you twist un, the top end comin' around. And when you pushed it into the rick, that would hold your rope to hold the thatch. When you put your thatch, this rope along, you'd spear it in. You'd have a rope comin' along - if you had a thatch roof as wide as this, say, you'd have about ten ropes which was speared in at the end, comin' along to hold your straw down. You had to have your straw lovely and straight for thatch, you know; so the water wouldn't go in. And as the rope was comin' along, then you'd stick these spears in. You always had to stick 'em straight in, or even lookin' a bit upwards; so the water would run out. Never stick downward, or else the water go down into the rick you see. And we used to do that - it would take you about a bloomin' day, or more, to do that.

We always used wheaten straw. We grew it long if we could. We used to have it thrashed same as our straw. In the old days, when they really took interest in thrashin', they used to make what they called reed. They had a reed-makin' machine in their barns. This was old-fashioned, could have done in the round house, I suppose.

152

And that one would just thrash out. You'd just put the heads in the drum to get the grain out; then you wouldn't damage the straw, you see; and it would stay lovely and straight. That would thatch beautiful. But ours used to go right through the drum. Some would get broken a bit, but it was still all right. That's what they used to do. I think they still make reed now fer these house thatchers. They still do reed corn because it damages the straw. I believe they have somethin' new, now, they use. Some sort of reeds they grow. I think so.

You know where the garage is at Whitecross, or was? There used to be a little thatch cottage on the corner there when we used to go to school. An old lady lived there called Mrs. Parsons. And that was before the garage was built, I am guessin', about at the beginning of the war. And she lived there before the war. And then she left, and it was knocked down, like, for the garage. That one was thatched.

And my father owned a little cob cottage in Lanreath, and he thatched it himself. Then it got condemned, not fit to live in after a few years. And then he had it knocked down and built a fresh one. He could get a grant for a fresh one. I think he had it rebuilt. I think he said it cost about £200, he thought. Heck of a lot of money. About two bedroom. They had a bathroom, a lovely sloped roof, for that money.

That's the one I can remember most in this parish, that little cottage on the corner. Because when I used to go to school, the old lady that was there used to ask me for a sweet turnip. And I used to go in the field at home and get one and carry it to school and get a penny. And that would buy a Kelly's ice cream.

I got two fields of silage now. I sold the grass, kept some back for silage. Two other farmers came and baled it for me. And they was only saying that they reckoned, that there was over a £100,000 worth of equipment in that field. The store tractors and one of them round balers and one of them things that wraps it and carries bales on their spikes. And they had a great big mower, a brand new one; and that was worth several thousand pounds. But they never touched a blade of grass nor lifted a bale from when they started to when they finished. Nothing was touched by hand. Everything they done from sitting on the tractor. All that they done by hand was put on new rolls of plastic on the wrappin' machine - that was the only bit of work that was done with their hands. Everything was done on the tractor. Well, they was two farmers, really. One had the baler and wrapper and the other the stacking thing and the carriers for carrying the bales, you know. I sold it to them, so much a bale.

Someone was telling me, the other day, a contractor came out to a farm. And he had a bloomin' great machine for doing silage - one of them that blows it into the trailer, I take it. And he come, and he done their farm, and then he went to another; and by the end of the day he'd done a hundred acres. Massive great thing he had. He had the same problem as you was saying about, that he couldn't get it in the gateways. Self propelled thing or something picks it up. And you know how they usually pick up two rows of cutter together. This one was takin' up six rows. They had to get six rows in, they ate it so fast. You can tell how fast they had to cart it away. I think they said it cost about £120,000.